THE TRIAL OF DON PEDRO LEÓN LUJÁN

# THE TRIAL
## OF DON PEDRO
## LEÓN LUJÁN

### THE ATTACK AGAINST
### INDIAN SLAVERY AND MEXICAN TRADERS IN UTAH

SONDRA JONES

THE UNIVERSITY OF UTAH PRESS
SALT LAKE CITY

© 2000 by the University of Utah Press
All rights reserved

Printed on acid-free paper

2005   2004   2003   2002   2001   2000

5   4   3   2   1

Library of Congress Cataloging-in-Publication Data

Jones, Sondra, 1949–
    The trial of Don Pedro León Luján : the attack against Indian
slavery and the Mexican traders in Utah / Sondra Jones.
        p.   cm.
    Includes bibliographical references (p.   ) and index.
    ISBN 0-87480-615-1 (alk. paper)
    1. Luján, Pedro León, b. 1794 Trials, litigation, etc.
2. Slavery—Law and legislation—Utah—History. 3. Trials—Utah—
Salt Lake City. 4. Slavery—New Mexico—History. 5. Slavery—
Utah—History. 6. Indians of North America—Legal status, laws,
etc.—Utah—History. 7. Indians of North America—Utah—Social
conditions.   I. Title.
KF223.L85J66   1999
306.3'62'09792—dc21                                              99-41534
                                                                  CIP

# CONTENTS

# ILLUSTRATIONS

# MAPS

# ACKNOWLEDGMENTS

A number of people and organizations helped make this work possible, and I would be remiss if I did not acknowledge them. Robert Westover, of the Brigham Young University Department of History, was an enthusiastic supporter of this project from its inception, as were others who later urged its publication, including Thomas Alexander and Fred Gowans; likewise, the History Department itself helped make some of the research in New Mexico possible through generous financial grants. I would also like to recognize the help provided me by the personnel at the LDS Church History Archives, the Utah State History Archives, the New Mexico State History Archives, the Museum of New Mexico, and the Archdiocese of New Mexico. Without the aid of these archivists I would have had a great deal more trouble finding some of the documents that gave depth to this study.

Last, but not least, I must acknowledge the patience, perseverance, and long suffering of my husband, Robert, and my children, who willingly put up with long trips to archives (and interminable historical narratives to a captive audience as I drove), as well as my idiosyncrasies and absent-mindedness when I was so frequently caught up in writing.

# Introduction

It was a lucrative trade, the capture and selling of Indian women and children. Many a man's fortune could be made in the trade, and not a few were willing to chance the occasional dangers the trade brought with it. Not only were there hazards in raiding Indian camps or traveling deep into Indian country to trade for the captives, but there was also the off-chance of being picked up by overzealous authorities for participating in the illegal business. Still, there was an eager market for the captives in New Mexico, and wherever there is a market for merchandise, illegal or not, there will always be suppliers. And if ongoing warfare was the result of such trade, so much the better for facilitating the acquisition of new captives and the making of new fortunes.

A long history of compulsory Indian labor in Spain's possessions in the New World, and especially in its frontier settlements like those in New Mexico, left the practice of dealing in Indian slaves and captives—illegal though it might have been—a thriving business. And Americans, caught up in the question of whether to extend Negro slavery through their new western acquisitions following the Mexican War and long catechized in the Black Legend of Spain's mistreatment of Indians, were not surprised to find it among Mexicans in New Mexico Territory.

Yet, contrary to the stereotypical image of New Mexico as a land replete with people of color as *slaves*, the practice of Indian *slavery* was illegal and had been for hundreds of years under both Spanish and Mexican jurisdiction. Because these Mexican laws were never changed under American rule, slavery continued to be illegal after the Mexican War brought New Mexico into the United States in 1848. And, in a political move to distance itself from its land-grabbing, slave-state neighbor, Texas, the hopeful New Mexican constitutional legislature would make a stand against black slavery as early as its 1848 bid for statehood.[1] It was the profligate use of Mexican peons and unwilling Indian indentures in temporary, compulsory pools of laborers, and especially the black market in Indian children for child-hungry frontier settlements, that Americans discovered in New Mexico, not the chattel slavery of their own southern states.

Ironically, it would be the territory of Utah, an enclave of independent-minded, freedom-loving, and religiously idealistic settlers, most of whose origins lay among northern abolitionists and Free-Soilers, that would remain the single western territory in which slavery was tolerated and remained legal. Abhorring the enslavement of Indian captives and their transportation to New Mexico, Utahns would nevertheless embrace a modified form of its practice among their own people, at the same time passing legislation to regulate the treatment (and thus accepting the existence) of the black slaves in their territory. It would not be for another ten years (1859) that the New Mexican territorial legislature, in response to the Dred Scott decision and the de facto extension of slavery throughout the entire United States, would formally recognize the existence of black slavery and pass its own regulations for the treatment, punishment, and recapture of black slaves.[2]

The early action of the Utah legislature came about because the colonizing Mormon pioneers found that they had chosen as their promised land a portion of frontier Mexico that had been for years the center of an active Indian slave trade, the apex and rendezvous point of the Mexican traders who plied the Old Spanish Trail between New Mexico, Utah, and California. In the fall of 1851 the newly created Utah Territory was in the process of organizing itself after its unsuccessful bid for statehood. Mormon pioneers had arrived in the valley of the Great Salt Lake only four years earlier. For the first several years, these Anglo settlers had contended mostly with nature in their attempts to establish themselves, for they had, by accident or design, settled in an Indian "no-man's" land; the valley lay in the extreme south of Shoshone territory and was north of traditional Ute country.[3]

Originally part of northern Mexico, much of Utah had been worked by fur trappers and Indian traders based in the frontier settlements of Taos, Abiquiú, and Santa Fe. But with the treaty of Guadalupe Hidalgo in 1848, the area became part of the United States and bound by the policies of that country. Two years later Utah and New Mexico territories were created as part of the Compromise of 1850 (one of Congress's ongoing attempts to reconcile northern and southern interests and the question of slavery). Utah and New Mexico were allowed to enter the Union, choosing for themselves whether they would be "slave" or "free," balancing the entrance of free California. The two territories split the region from the crest of the Rocky Mountains to the borders of California, and from the forty-second parallel to the new border of Mexico.

When many of the newly appointed, non-Mormon (gentile) government officials fled Utah in September 1851, Mormon officials stepped in to assume (or reassume) responsibilities. One of the major areas the new territory needed to deal with was Indian relations; new Mormon colonies had already begun to spread south into Ute strongholds in the Utah and Sanpete valleys by 1849, and late 1850 saw new colonizing and missionary efforts as far as Parowan, two hundred miles south of Great Salt Lake City. Governor Brigham Young would even choose a location deep in central Utah as the site of the proposed new territorial capital.

Although lobbying for Indian removal was being carried on in Washington, difficulties concomitant with settling in the midst of Indian lands needed to be dealt with immediately. Removal—if it could be obtained—would extinguish Indian title to the land, making the legality of Mormon settlements unquestioned, but the federal government seemed in no hurry to act.[4] In the meantime, however, Mormon settlements were threatened by the continuing presence of the warlike Ute Indians, who demanded or begged food, carried on intertribal conflicts, and demanded purchasers for their Indian captives. Brigham Young would attempt to shift the responsibility for the Indians from Mormon to federal shoulders. But, for the time being, the Indians were a major element of pioneer life, and their activities heavily influenced Mormon settlement policies.

Ironically, it was another European-based society that had most significantly affected the behavior of these Utah Indians. The Mormons early discovered that their settlements lay along the Old Spanish Trail, in the midst of an active trade between Utes and Mexicans. Central Utah had been the destination for Mexican traders for over fifty years, and for twenty years more had continued to be a significant stop even after this trail extended into California. Though mules, buckskins, and woven cloth were important to the New Mexico–California traders, the staple of the Indian trade in central Utah was, and had been for decades, captive Indian women and children who were in demand in Hispanic households as "indentured" menial servants.[5] Although they did not necessarily condemn slavery per se, the Mormons, newly planted in Utah, considered the trade reprehensible on both moral and political counts and sought a variety of means to extinguish it. When the Trade and Intercourse Act of 1834, regulating Indian relations, was extended over the new territories in 1851, Mormon officials found the tool they needed for combating the Mexican trade they so disliked.

In December 1851 authorities from Manti, Utah, arrested eight "Spanish" traders from New Mexico,[6] including their leader, "Pedro León" Luján,[7] and eventually brought them to trial in the First Judicial Court of Utah Territory in Great Salt Lake City. They were accused of violating the laws regulating the trade and traffic with Indian tribes (the Trade and Intercourse Act of 1834), having allegedly traded with the Ute Indians for nine Indian slaves (a woman and eight children). After a four-day trial they were found guilty of trading illegally with the Indians; fined the mandatory five hundred dollars, to be paid from the sale of their confiscated goods; and, despite a number of appeals and countersuits, eventually returned, disgruntled, to New Mexico. There they continued their appeals as high as the office of the commissioner of Indian affairs in Washington, D.C.

The arrest and trial became something of a cause célèbre in Utah, forcing a closer examination of several thorny problems plaguing the new territory. Among these problems were the questions of what constituted "Indian country" and the legality of Mormon trade with the Indians if Utah were to be considered "Indian country," the control of trade within Utah territorial boundaries, the legality of the enslavement of Indians, and, especially, what to do with the prevalent, though repugnant, Indian slave trade in which the Mormons found themselves active participants.

In essence, *United States v. Pedro León et al.* became a test case for crystallizing certain judicial and legislative policies in Utah Territory. It was politically and morally expedient that the trading by outsiders for the purpose of transporting Indian captives away from Utah be made officially illegal—as long as a legal mechanism remained that allowed Mormon settlers to continue to absorb the market in Indian children. Therefore, a precedent had to be set barring the perennial New Mexican traders from Utah where they could stir up trouble with the Indians. It was also critically important to attempt to stop the warfare between Indian tribes caused by the raiding for captives to sell, warfare that threatened Mormon settlements and missionary efforts. Thus, although Brigham Young reportedly used his influence during the Mexicans' trial to ensure that it was fair, the widespread prejudice against Mexicans as well as the political necessity of a guilty verdict almost certainly influenced the outcome. The Pedro León incident—Utah histories and the court documents consistently referred to him as simply Pedro León—has all but faded into short references or footnotes in Utah's history, if it is noted at all. But it was a most important case at the time and led directly to several pieces of legislation that would have lasting effects on Utah, as well as New Mexico.

It also played a major role in causing at least one major Indian war and was a contributory factor to a second. It is not surprising in our enlightened age of concern for human rights that the child-slaver Pedro León has come down to us painted in the black hues of villainy, his defense referred to sneeringly as the excuses of an unscrupulous trader in flagrant disregard for authority and morality, his punishment the just deserts of a sordid dealer in human flesh. But, on closer examination, the court records and depositions of the trial reveal a very different interpretation of this page in Utah and western history. And a clearer picture of the Pedro León affair emerges when it is placed in its historical and cultural context, not only the political and cultural milieu of early Mormon Utah but also the cultural and historical background of the New Mexican frontier and of Indian slavery itself.

The trial of Pedro León is a classic example of a mixture of racial, cultural, and religious bias, along with the clashing of cultural perspectives. Both sides believed they were justified in their actions. Since the Anglo-Mormon perspective is probably more familiar to most modern Americans, it has been easy to accept that version of the Pedro León incident. But there is another perspective, and to understand it, it is necessary to look at the Spanish tradition of forced Indian servitude, particularly in New Mexico, and the tradition of Indian trading on the New Mexican frontier. It is also necessary to know who exactly Pedro León Luján was, not only as a product of his culture and his society but as an individual with a position and unique experiences within that society. And, obliquely, it is necessary to understand the role of the Ute Indians within the context of the slave-trading tradition, as well as their individual roles in the incident and the trial and their responses to the trial's results.

The Mexicans' defense has only occasionally been referred to by historians, and then dismissed as false. Fully accepting the verdict of the court, scholars have failed to examine the affidavits and petitions filed in defense of the Mexicans or entertain the possibility that the Mexicans were telling the truth in explaining the presence of their Indian captives and their reasons for delaying their departure from Utah. Instead, historians have sketched a picture of Pedro León as defiantly refusing to leave before trading for slaves and, when caught and punished, departing the territory in a vengeful rage while stirring up Indians against the Mormons along the way.

This picture is, however, flawed. It is my purpose to reexamine the events of 1851–52 in order to produce a more accurate depiction of Don Pedro León Luján, his arrest and trial, and his subsequent behavior.

I begin by reviewing the history of Indian slavery, including the institution of forced Indian servitude in Hispanic New Mexico, the market demand for it, its justification, and its political and cultural effects. I also examine the cultural and political environment in Mormon-dominated Utah in 1851–52, especially in terms of the Mormons' attitudes toward slavery, both Negro and Indian. In addition, I explore the traditions of the Ute Indians with whom the Spanish and Mexicans traded and their role in fostering and maintaining the Indian slave trade, as well as the effect on them of its termination.

Finally, and most important, I examine the court records of the trial of "Pedro León et al." in order to create a clearer picture of the incident itself through the testimonies and affidavits of the men involved, their legal responses, court arguments, and post-trial petitions. An analysis of the proceedings and the participants' responses, coupled with a cultural and political understanding of the times and the men involved, should help us better comprehend what really happened at the trial of Don Pedro León Luján.

## CHAPTER ONE

# The Evolution of a Stereotype and the Devolution of Indian History in Utah

The arrest, trial, and expulsion of Mexican traders and its role in inciting the 1853 Walker Indian War has become a standard, if only minor, notation in Utah history.[1] Generally, it falls under a chapter or subheading such as "Indian Relations"; it is frequently discussed as an antecedent to the Walker War, and it is portrayed as the righteous triumph of Mormon officials and their courts over the immoral traditions of Mexicans and Indians, clearing the way for colonization and the expansion of white settlements—civilization—in Utah. This is understandable, since the references used by early historians, and subsequently cited by succeeding historians, were all contemporary, Anglo-Mormon sources.

The incident may also be discussed in its context as part of the Indian slaving tradition or as part of Mormon attempts to proselytize and assimilate the Indian. Other than these short references to "Indian history," the episode involving Pedro León Luján and his Mexican traders has been little studied, and the growth of the stereotype of the villainous and greedy Mexican who deliberately flouted Utah laws and heinously tried to instigate an Indian war against Anglo-Americans—has been accepted, assimilated, and finally adopted as fact, and has begun to be relegated to the footnotes of an increasingly white-oriented history of Utah.

Unfortunately, that is not quite what happened. It is true that by the end of his experiences in Utah, Luján had become embittered against the Mormons in Utah and may have had a hand with other traders in stirring up the Indians later because his years-long trade had been legally and decisively stopped. Nevertheless, he began the story with earnest attempts not to flout but to follow the letter of the trade laws so recently imposed on him and other Mexicans as a result of the Mexican War and the sudden acquisition of frontier Mexico—New Mexico, Utah, and California territories—by the United States.

The 1851 episode in which Luján was arrested, tried, and expelled from Utah started as a peaceful request from the trader for an extension or renewal of his trade license from the acting Indian superintendent in Utah Territory, Brigham Young, whom he had sought and finally caught up with in Sanpete Valley. When the license was refused and the traders lectured on the evils of Indian slavery, Luján agreed to leave the territory after securing supplies for the return trip. But the Indians had other ideas. Stock was stolen and Indian children and one woman were offered or thrust on the traders in compensation by Ute slavers who suggested they take them or leave them as they liked. Caught with the evidence of their "trading" without a license, the Mexicans were arrested, tried twice, and, despite appeals, eventually expelled, without incident, from the territory. No major trading expeditions arrived in Utah in 1852 (Luján was just returning to New Mexico then), but in 1853 New Mexican traders returned, this time openly belligerent and defiant of the Mormon laws and officials. But this slaving caravan was led not by Luján—except perhaps as a guide and servant—but by a bellicose Anglo-American by the name of Dr. C. A. W. Bowman. These men openly traded weapons and provoked Indian hostilities toward the Mormon settlers in response to what had happened in 1851–52 and in order to demonstrate that their freedom to trade would not be impinged on by the Utah Mormons. And it was these dangerous activities that impelled Brigham Young to issue military orders to seek out, arrest, and expel all Mexican trading parties in the territory.

Unfortunately from a historical sense, since both the 1851 and 1853 trading expeditions sought to purchase Indian captives to sell in New Mexico and were involved in some type of official confrontation, the peaceful, judicial episode with Luján's traders in 1851–52 has consistently but inaccurately been wedded with the decidedly nonpeaceful affair in 1853. This historical telescoping of events, not to mention a sometimes jumbled and inaccurate chronicling of the affair, has perpetuated an erroneous and prejudicial portrayal of the 1851 arrest and trial of Luján and his companions. As a result, Luján has been vilified as responsible, along with all Mexican traders, for inciting Indian troubles and being obnoxiously belligerent and defiant from the beginning of the Mormon period. In a topsy-turvy reverse chronology, this "dangerous" situation has then been cited by many historians as the original compelling reason for fighting Indian slavery and arresting Luján in the first place.

On the contrary, Mormon concern about the trade in 1851 lay in its perceived immorality, its inciting of intertribal Indian wars (in order to gather slaves), and its interference with Mormon settlements. The Mormons disliked the Mexican traders because they perpetuated these problems by providing a ready market for the small captives the Ute slavers sold. But up until 1853 Mexican traders had plied their trade peacefully. It was only after the arrest and expulsion of Luján and his traders and the passing of laws against slave trading that the trouble with the Mexicans began. The truth of the matter is that the belligerence of the 1853 traders was not the cause but the result of Don Pedro León's arrest and the passing of anti–Indian slavery laws.

The contemporary sources on the affair were highly prejudiced against the Mexicans, because they *were* Mexican and particularly because they dealt in the Indian slave trade. It is these sources that early historians used to assemble the Pedro León story.

The major contemporary sources on Indian slavery and the Pedro León affair include statements (generally denunciations of the trade) by Brigham Young, governor and ex officio superintendent of Indian affairs in Utah at the time as well as leader of the Mormon church, and reports or editorials appearing in the only Utah newspaper then being published, the *Deseret News Weekly*, a paper with a decidedly Anglo-Mormon perspective.[2] Most often cited is a condemnatory editorial by Willard Richards, published November 15, 1851, which describes the Mexican trading party when it was first encountered, Mormon attitudes toward it, and the trade itself. The paper also published the court findings, on March 6, 1852, and Young's addresses to the legislature.

The New Mexican references to the Pedro León case are found only in the trader's complaints and appeals to Washington, made in 1852 from New Mexico through sympathetic officials there. But if any other reports of it were ever published in New Mexico newspapers presenting a New Mexican perspective, they have been lost, and the only non-Mormon publication ever to comment on Utah's actions against New Mexican traders was a Mexican newspaper that editorialized on the expulsion of all (New) Mexican traders a year later, in 1853.[3]

The Utah legislature's preamble to its acts for the relief of Indian prisoners is another frequently referenced contemporary source. Its denunciation of Indian slavery (and Indian and Mexican slavers) provided Utah its justification for enacting the Indian indenturing laws.[4]

Daniel Jones's biographical account of his time among the Indians, published in 1890, is an additional source frequently quoted on the Pedro León and Bowman incidents.[5] Jones, a Mormon, was an interpreter for Indians and occasionally for Mexicans and an eyewitness to the events involving Luján and his traders, as well as subsequent events. He was writing in retrospect, however, relying on his memory of incidents that had occurred years earlier; consequently, he made errors, placing the confrontation between Young and Luján in Provo rather than near Manti, for example, and combining the autumn 1851 episode with the Bowman affair in April 1853—an error that would be perpetuated by later historians.

A brief chronological review of how the case has been dealt with by historians illustrates how Luján's stereotype has developed; peripherally, it also shows the interesting trend of current historians to relegate Indian affairs in general to all but marginal references in Utah histories. This is unfortunate, since Mormon-Indian relations were significant (and sometimes pivotal) in the evolution and shaping of Utah's early history and should not be so easily dismissed.

Most historians have chosen to discuss the Pedro León incident as one of the causes of the 1853 Walker War. In his *History of Utah* (1889) Hubert Howe Bancroft refers to the Mexican trading incident as "among the causes" of the war, since such trading parties supplied guns, ammunition, and horses to the Indians and "often" received captives in exchange. He goes on to claim that because of the frequency and presence of traders, in 1853 Young finally ordered the arrest of all "strolling bands of Mexicans." Laws were subsequently passed, he continues, to "induce the brethren" to purchase children who would otherwise be bought by the Mexicans or abandoned by their parents.[6] Bancroft was apparently unaware that this advice had actually been given by Brigham Young a year before the Pedro León incident and was legalized afterward only as a consequence of the court proceedings.

Orson F. Whitney's *History of Utah* has one of the more extensive discussions of the Pedro León incident, including several pages on the activity of Mexican traders in Utah and quotations from the *Deseret News Weekly*'s editorials and published court proceedings. It is this history, however, that truly begins the welding of the two disparate incidents. Like Bancroft, Whitney wants to lay the groundwork for explaining the Walker War: The "restless and belligerent" Ute chief, Walker, was considered to be "at the bottom of the trouble," which ended in the war, but was only the "visible hand," the major cause of the war being "other agencies . . . at work inciting him to hostility"—specifically, the Mexican traders, beginning with

Luján. Unfortunately, and perhaps influenced by Jones's account, Whitney mixes the 1851 and 1853 events, placing the belligerent leader of the 1853 trading expedition, Dr. Bowman, with the peaceful Luján caravan of 1851. Consequently, Whitney erroneously implies that it was because of aggressive and threatening behavior on the part of Luján and his traders, in addition to their having traded for captives in defiance of official warnings, that they were arrested and brought to court.[7] This error would be perpetuated by subsequent historians.

A good example of this growing stereotype occurs in a local history published thirty years later by J. Marinus Jensen. Jensen inaccurately accuses Luján of directly "fanning" the "smoldering ill-will" of the Indians while trading for Indian slaves in 1851. Warnings to "desist" were treated by Luján "with impudence and contempt," until "finally" he and his companions were arrested. A brief reference to Young's dispatching of the militia in April 1853 to arrest slave traders is the only allusion to the Bowman incident. Like Whitney, Jensen telescopes the two events, attributing the actions of a belligerent Dr. Bowman and his traders to Luján's earlier, peaceful caravan.[8]

Similarly, the influential historian L. H. Creer perpetuates errors and further muddles the events in his 1929 text, *Utah and the Nation*:

> These protests and warnings had no effect upon the slave traders, who declared that they would do as they pleased regardless of law and authority [1853]; whereupon Pedro León and seven of his men were arrested and tried before a justice of the peace at Manti [1851]. . . . [After the trial] the Mexicans were again ordered to leave the territory [1851], avenged themselves by stirring up the savages against the settlers [1853]. They furnished the Indians with guns and ammunition, contrary to the laws of the United States [1853].[9]

Creer's 1947 text, *The Founding of an Empire*, and an article on the Great Basin slave trade naturally repeat the errors of his previous book, continuing to amalgamate the activities of Luján and Bowman in order to establish the Mormon case against Mexican traders, and Luján in particular.[10] Creer inaccurately portrays the Utahns' "profound shock" at the slave trade as the motivation for Brigham

Young's 1853 proclamation against "strolling" Mexicans in order to end the "whole sordid business." Although it was Utah's distaste for the slave trade that initiated actions to make the trade illegal in 1851–52, it was Dr. Bowman's challenge to the new laws and the threat of an Indian war that motivated Young's proclamation and militia action against the traders a year later, in 1853.

Creer's opinion of the traders as "unscrupulous" and vengeful hardens into fact the typical, though inaccurate, historical stereotype of Luján and all Mexican traders. At the same time, Creer succeeds in casting the Mormons in the heroic role of the fearless abolitionists who were willing to take action against the traders despite its resulting in Indian hostility and war.

It is an interesting side note to see that in 1929 Creer specifically writes that Utah "legaliz[ed] Indian slavery," in reference to the Indian indenturing act of 1852. Apparently, the difference between slavery and indenturing remained a fine line, with some historians continuing to view indenturing as slavery, including those in Utah. Thirty-five years later Gustive O. Larson would echo Creer in a rather contradictory statement "that the legislature [legalized] Indian slavery," making it possible for Mormons to "rescue scores of native youth from the evils of slavery,"[11] and L. R. Bailey would write in his study of Indian slavery that "slavery had been virtually legalized" in Utah in 1852.[12]

Other historians writing about the Indian slave trade and early Spanish and Mexican exploration and trade in the Great Basin used the Whitney history as their major source along with some of the standard contemporary documents to detail the slave trade[13] or show how it led to the 1853 Indian war in Utah.[14] By the 1930s Don Pedro León had become simply an explanatory note to the Walker War.

When B. H. Roberts discusses the Pedro León case in *History of the Church* (1930), it is only in reference to its effect on Indian hostilities and the 1853 Walker War. Following Whitney, Roberts cites the arrest of the Mexican traders and the interdiction of the slave trade as the underlying cause of that war rather than the usurpation of Indian lands, which other historians have begun to recognize was an important factor as well. The incident that sparked the war (the accidental killing of an Indian by a Mormon settler) "was not the real cause of the war, but merely a pretext for beginning hostilities," Roberts writes. He goes on to describe the custom of Indian slavery and the annual Mexican slave-trading expeditions, citing Richards's *Deseret News Weekly* editorial that condemned the "dastardly business" and quoting

Brigham Young's legislative address in which he denounced the Mexican defendants as having been "determined to carry on their nefarious traffic." Reference is also made to Young's later charge in 1853 that the traders had "poisoned the minds of the Indians." Roberts concludes that "the suppression then of the slave trade . . . and the evil counsels and influence of the slave traders among them, as a consequence of that suppression, may be set down as the cause of the Indian disturbances . . . and not the unfortunate Springville incident."[15] (Which was a neat way, certainly, of exonerating the Mormons of all culpability in causing the war and laying it directly on the shoulders of the Mexican traders instead.) Since Roberts makes no mention of the second, belligerent trip by Mexican traders in 1853, the implication is that the Indians were stirred up by Luján's traders immediately after their trial in January 1852, with the effective culmination being the war begun in 1853.

A. L. Neff's history of Utah, published in 1940, bypasses the Pedro León incident completely, discussing only Bowman's Mexican traders who came into Utah trading arms for children in 1853. But a footnote provided by his editor, L. H. Creer, supplies the missing background information on the slave trade, the indenturing act, and the Pedro León incident; of course, Creer perpetuates the same errors he made in his own texts in which the Dr. Bowman and Pedro León incidents are bundled together, once again leaving an inaccurate portrayal of both episodes.[16]

Milton R. Hunter's 1943 history of Utah contains no mention of Luján or Mexican traders and makes only peripheral references to the problem of Indian slavery, and his rather ethnocentric 1946 book, *Utah: The Story of Her People*, contains no references to Utah's Indian population at all![17] In his 1943 history the problem of the slave trade is noted only in passing, as are the attempts to counteract it through the indenture law and the proclamation to arrest all "strolling parties" of Mexicans. Hunter, too, notes that one of several causes of the Walker War was the attempt to stop the slave trade, which incited the Mexicans to seek revenge by supplying Indians with arms, ammunition, and a motive (lost lands) for hostilities. (Do we assume that Indians hadn't noticed the loss before the traders pointed it out to them? The Provo Indian War of 1850 would argue otherwise.)

Gustive O. Larson's 1952 article on the Ute chief Wákara includes both the Pedro León and Dr. Bowman incidents, but with the usual number of inaccuracies. Larson predates the laws against Indian slavery to before the arrest of the traders (justifying their arrest) and incorrectly writes that Young "found" Pedro León and his trading party and that the trader was "taken into custody, together with his slave property." He includes the often recounted tale of the brutal killing of a child by Arapeen (Wákara's kin brother), who blamed the child's death on the Mormons for stopping the Mexican trade while not buying the captives themselves. Larson erroneously claims, however, that Arapeen's brutality was in response to Luján's expulsion (1852) instead of the result of the enforcement of the anti–slave-trading edicts and expulsion of Bowman's traders in 1853, which it was. Later, in his relation of the Bowman incident, he incorrectly writes that "the frustrated Spaniards stirred [the Indians] up against the Mormons *as Pedro León had done previously*" (emphasis added) (he hadn't).[18]

LeRoy and Ann Hafen's *Old Spanish Trail* (1954) gives one the most impartial renditions of the Pedro León case, quoting extensively from the court findings, Daniel Jones, and the Utah legislature. This work also includes an affidavit submitted in New Mexico for Luján by Lafayette Head (who would later be a Ute Indian agent in Colorado) which defends Luján by denying the existence of a trade in "slaves" and describing the trade as a system of Hispanic fostering instead.[19]

Another impartial reference to the trial can be found in a recent study (1997) by Joseph P. Sánchez of explorers, traders, and slavers on the Old Spanish Trail and their role in blazing an important immigrant route to California. Like others who have examined the trading trail, Sánchez refers to the Pedro León incident, but only to illustrate the hostility of Mormons toward the traditional Mexican trade and their interdiction of it after 1852. He cites the court's summary "Information" published in the *Deseret News Weekly* and Young's proclamation against Mexican traders (instigated by the Bowman incident, he notes, without referring to Bowman or his aide, Luján), both collected secondarily from other studies of Spanish and Mexican exploration in the Great Basin. Significantly, Sánchez adds that contemporaries of Luján were also rebuffed and made complaints that the interdiction was due to the Mormons' desire to "dominate" the Ute trade themselves—a complaint that was actually made by Luján himself to the superintendent of Indian Affairs in New Mexico.[20]

Paul Bailey's romantic biography of Wákara (1954) is only passably credible in its treatment of the Mexican traders. Bailey erroneously depicts the Mexicans and the Utes as "transacting a lively business" when Brigham Young arrived in Sanpete Valley. His Utes are "first surprised" and then "angered" when Young immediately orders the Mexicans' arrest and removal to Salt Lake for trial "under provision of the new slave-trade act." Actually, the traders had not begun to trade since they were still seeking Young to renew their license; they were not immediately arrested (that was six weeks later); they could not be tried under a "new" slave-trade act since that law was not passed until after their trial in January of 1852; and the Indians were "surprised" and "angered" not at the traders' arrest but at the traders' refusal to trade with them later. In 1851 their anger was not directed at Mormons, as Bailey implies, but at the traders, from whom they stole horses and against whom they would later testify at the trial. (This attitude would change by 1853.)[21]

Bailey also incorrectly describes the Dr. Bowman affair in 1853 when he writes that Bowman tried to trade at Provo, where "the militia picked him up, and then sped a detachment south to round up his associates." Bowman did deliberately encounter Brigham Young at Provo but was never "picked up," although he did inspire Young to send the militia south to find other Mexican traders. None was encountered outside Utah Valley; however, locals in Sanpete Valley temporarily restrained Bowman's traders and then released them, and the Southern Utah settlements briefly jailed others.

Eight years later Conway B. Sonne took a more scholarly look at Wákara.[22] Nevertheless, his book, though more impartial than Bailey's, contains inaccuracies. According to his narrative, Brigham Young only heard of the traders and immediately issued orders for their arrest on December 13, 1851 (actually, Manti officials arrested and tried the traders on their own, and Judge Snow ordered them retried in Great Salt Lake City six weeks after they had first approached Young personally for licenses). Sonne writes that eight were arrested but only Pedro León was indicted and tried (all were tried as Pedro León et al.). He also erroneously notes that slavery was illegal in United States territories and that Utah would formally outlaw it in 1852. In actuality, the Compromise of 1850 left that decision up to all new territories entering the Union after the war with Mexico, and Utah outlawed only the enslavement of Indians, while continuing to allow Negro slavery up to the time of the Thirteenth Amendment fifteen years later.

Gustive O. Larson's 1965 *Outline History of Utah and the Mormons* treats the Indian slave trade and Luján briefly prior to, though not in connection with, the

Walker War. But like most Utah historians, Larson perpetuates the story that Brigham Young stumbled on the traders while their trade was in full swing, that he ordered them from the territory at that time, and that they were forced to release their captives. Actually, the captives were not freed but confiscated along with the traders' goods when Luján and his party were arrested later, and the court had to determine their status as property to be sold to pay their fine or as free persons to be given into indentures. And like previous historians, Larson telescopes the events of 1851–52 and 1853 when he repeats Creer's accusations against Luján of "aveng[ing] himself by supplying firearms to the natives and stirring them up against the Mormons" immediately after the trial.[23]

L. R. Bailey's 1966 study of Indian slavery in the Southwest includes an extensive chapter on the Utah slave trade and the Pedro León incident. Since the book makes no secret of its opinion of the slave trade, it is no surprise to find Luján denigrated as one of the few Mexican traders who dared the "wrath of the Mormon 'lion'" and traded in "flagrant disregard of Mormon authority."[24]

But once again history is garbled as events are taken out of sequence. Bailey depicts Brigham Young as "aroused" by the slave-trading situation and "vowing" to halt the "insidious traffic" (probably true); in order to do so, he "sought out New Mexican traders" (not true, both Luján and Dr. Bowman sought him out) to explain that they could no longer trade. Luján is described as defying Young by not leaving the territory immediately (he had received permission from Mormon officials to buy supplies for the trip home and later to pursue some Indians who had stolen stock). Stating that León's traders were apprehended shortly after entering the territory (actually more than six weeks after meeting with Brigham Young), Bailey gives the impression that the captives had been acquired before any contact with whites was made, again inaccurate. He also misidentifies the Indians who stole the Mexicans' horses as Paiutes, although he indicates no source for his information; but those Indians who were identified in affidavits, as well as those who testified, were Ute. Perhaps he only assumed they must be Paiute because they ate the stolen horses instead of riding them![25]

Bailey remarks, however, that "not only were León and his party badly treated by Mormons . . . but other New Mexicans suffered as well from the iron will of Brigham Young," thus acknowledging the stringent policy specifically directed against Mexicans by the Mormons. Bailey recognizes that the thrust of the antislavery laws was against Mexican trade in particular, not just the trade in Indian captives (Mormons continued to barter for the children), despite the fact that the law only specified "slave-traders" and that since "slavery had been virtually legalized the previous year [1852, in Utah], . . . [it] could not be suppressed." Therefore, the military reconnaissance sent by Brigham Young in 1853 was not intended to stop the slave trade per se but was "founded in the desire to stamp out the flow of contraband weapons and ammunition which were being brought into Utah by New Mexican traders."[26] Bailey also notes the connection between the Walker War and the interdiction of Mexican trade when he writes flamboyantly that Wákara became angered at the Mormons when "Brigham . . . turned upon the 'Hawk' like a rabid dog—severing the arteries which supplied his life blood" (that is, the sale of captives and occasional tribute laid on Mexican caravans).[27]

Lyman Tyler's chapter on Indian history in *Utah's History*, edited in 1989 by Richard D. Poll and others, contains that text's only brief allusion to the Pedro León incident. As in earlier histories, the case is referred to as but "another clash" between Mormons and Utes leading to the Walker War. But in a misleading statement, Tyler states that Luján presented a license authorizing "them to engage in slave trading" (the license made no mention of slaves). Tyler goes on to imply that because the Indians tried to force trade thereafter, Young advised, and the legislature passed, laws to legalize the purchase and care of Indian children.[28] But Young had already been advocating their purchase, and forcible sales to Mormons had been taking place since 1847. Indeed, the indenturing laws were passed on the heels of Luján's trial; because Indians continued to offer children for sale, the trial merely *legalized* the inevitable purchase of Indian children, at the same time keeping their technical slavery (and thus the Mexican slave trade) illegal.

Unfortunately, the more recent histories of Utah are tending to deal more and more cursorily with the whole question of Indian slavery and early Mormon-Indian relations. Their oversimplification of the events continues to perpetuate the inaccurate picture history has drawn of the Mexican traders and the events leading to the closing of Mexican trade, and of Indian history itself in Utah.

For example, S. George Ellsworth's high school history texts, *Utah's Heritage* (1977) and *The New Utah's Heritage* (1985, rev. 1992), only briefly refer to the Pedro León incident: "One trader, arrested and forced to free some Indian slaves, took revenge by supplying firearms and ammunition to the Indians and stirring them up against the Mormons." This is followed by a two-line reference to the new anti–Indian slavery laws and the hostilities they aroused among the Indians.[29]

And Dean L. May's *Utah: A Peoples History*, a 1987 text created from an educational television series, ignores the Pedro León incident completely, referring only incidentally to Indian slavery and indenturing as one of the ways in which Mormons tried to assimilate the natives. Truncating events even further, May implies that the indenturing laws were passed as a direct result of the forcible sale of an Indian girl to Mormons in the winter of 1848–49: "Shortly thereafter" Brigham Young urged the purchase of Indian children "as a relief and benefit" to them and "to help the process of civilizing the natives." May notes, however, that regardless of the original benevolent intent, "no doubt" the practice sometimes more resembled "an indentured servitude than a 'purchase into freedom.'"[30]

It would be interesting to speculate about the trend in Utah histories to include fewer and more summary discussions of the impact of Indian relations on early Utah history. Apparently, even Indian relations, let alone the incident with Pedro León Luján and his stereotyped, "dastardly" Mexican traders, are becoming footnotes to a white history of the state.

## CHAPTER TWO

## THE INDIAN SLAVE TRADE IN NEW MEXICO

An understanding of the trade in Indian captives in New Mexico can only begin with an understanding of the long-standing tradition of Indian slavery, as it was practiced and justified not only by the European conquerors but by the Indians themselves.

### ENSLAVEMENT OF AMERICAN INDIANS

The traffic in captive Indian labor did not begin with the advent of Europeans in the Americas. Nevertheless, the Europeans who came to the Americas created large new markets for slaves, and the normal flow of captives was increased until slaving became a means unto itself for many Indians. Europeans also brought new twists on the traditional practices of captive labor, in particular the concept of chattel ownership.

#### INDIAN ENSLAVEMENT OF INDIANS

The enslavement of captives was an integral part of the warfare traditions of American Indians. Most early European explorers commented on the presence among Indian tribes of Indian slaves (*slave* was often synonymous with *prisoner*, or anything else that depended on a master for sustenance, such as a dog). In many cases obtaining captives became a motive for war itself. For example, Captain John Smith noted that Powhatan's tribe near Jamestown, Virginia, made war "not for lands and goods, but for women and children, whom they put not to death, but kept as captives, in which captivity they were made to do service."[1] Sometimes slave raids were so extensive that whole villages were obliterated. So frequently were the Pawnee Indians raided from both sides of the Mississippi River that although this extensive tribe was not destroyed, the term "Pawnee" became synonymous with "Indian slave."[2] Slavery was especially prevalent along the highly developed and wealthy Indians of the Pacific Northwest, where one journalist noted that Queen Charlotte Island formed "the great slave mart" of the Northwest coast, and large numbers of slaves were owned by tribal leaders.[3]

Women and children were those typically enslaved, whereas men or warriors were killed. In many cases enslavement was an alternative to the torture and death of Indian vengeance or hatred—a choice often made by women or tribal councils—with that alternative being used to instill disciplinary fear into the captives. Southern Indians often maimed or marked their captives by cutting their feet or severing tendons to keep them from running away or to track them easily if they did.

Although most captives were originally the result of warfare and were not generally considered trade goods, as European articles entered the commercial network a more active trade in war captives developed among Indian tribes. Captives were often bartered between tribes, so that Florida Indians, for example, could be found among tribes as far away as the Illinois Indians. Coronado used as guides two slaves from "Quivira" (on the plains) living in New Mexico and met another slave from the country de Soto was then traversing near the Mississippi.

Captives were frequently taken in order to wreak vengeance on an enemy tribe. Since the torturing and killing of enemy captives was also common,[4] some early explorers and missionaries reported purchasing captives to save their lives; indeed, early Jesuit and French missionaries "advocated . . . purchasing Indian captives by the traders in order to prevent their being put to death," and incidentally, to Christianize and develop guides and interpreters by so doing.[5] Captives could be used as a medium of exchange along with wampum and furs. As property, they could also be given as gifts (and were sometimes tendered to Europeans as such), exchanged for prisoners, or used to placate their enemies, win favor with others (especially whites), or as war reparations. In one case Indians near Detroit offered to raid distant tribes to provide slaves to give the French to "replace their dead."[6] Raids could also be made for the specific purpose of obtaining prisoners to replace the dead of their own tribe.

Indian slaves were generally used as domestic servants or field hands, or for hunting, fishing, or other menial jobs, including mining among the Cenis Indians. Women, of course, could also be used as mistresses or secondary wives. Treatment varied with circumstances and could be very mild or heavy-handed. Slaves who outlived their usefulness could be abandoned or simply killed and tossed aside. Enslavement carried a stigma, even when a prisoner was returned to his or her tribe; among most groups, however, Indian servants could work or marry their way out of servitude, and children of Indian captives did not (with some exceptions) inherit their parents' enslavement.

The enslavement of Indians by Europeans, while mirroring many of the Indian practices, brought its own variations.

### EUROPEAN ENSLAVEMENT OF INDIANS

For political reasons, the Spaniards were excoriated by other Europeans through the "Black Legend," which proclaimed the savage brutality of Spaniards toward Indians. Through disease, wars of extermination, and enslavement, Indians had been decimated by the millions in Spanish provinces. Nevertheless, the conquest, extermination, and enslavement of Indians was hardly limited to the Spaniards. Some of the worst scenes of cruelty and open wars of extermination were fought by the Russians in Alaska and by the Dutch and English on the eastern coast of North America. The enslavement of natives was practiced by all European nations.[7] Although the French are considered the most benevolent of the Europeans in their early relations with Indians, even their *coureurs de bois*, independent traders, traveled among the Indians bartering for whatever commodities—including Indian slaves—that they could trade in the French or English colonies. In 1707 La Salle presaged later complaints in New Mexico when he wrote that the *coureurs de bois* from Canada were "thus stirring up the Indian tribes against each other, in order to obtain Indian slaves to sell in Louisiana."[8] Other Europeans took like profits from intertribal—and general—Indian hostilities.

The Spanish, however, felt particularly justified in their subjugation of native Americans. For them, the stage had been set for Indian slavery forty years before the discovery of the Americas when Pope Nicholas V decreed that Catholic monarchs could sell all heathens and "foes of Christ" into slavery. Though he was specifically referring to the Muslims against whom Christians battled in the crusading spirit of the *Reconquista* of the Iberian peninsula, later popes came to interpret his mandate to mean *all* captives taken in religious wars.[9] This interpretation would have a number of ramifications. Eventually, not only heathens and non-Christians were sold into slavery but even Protestant Europeans were enslaved by Spanish warships.[10]

One of the most significant ramifications of Catholic acceptance of the papal edict was how it directed treatment by Spain of the millions of Indians who came under Spanish rule in the Americas. The European attitude toward Indians had been manifested as early as Columbus's first voyage when, in lieu of the lucrative gold or spices he had expected to find and which would have justified this and subsequent voyages, the captain returned with Caribbean Indian slaves instead.[11]

Indeed, all the European nations that looked to the Americas saw colonization as a commercial enterprise from which a profit could be made. Kings sought profit from tribute in some form or another, businessmen at home invested money expecting a return, and the first emissaries were, for the most part, men of the aristocratic class—usually second or third sons without an inheritance—who hoped to build estates in America without sullying their own hands with work. As Viceroy Luis de Velasco complained in 1608, "No one comes to the Indies to plow and sow, but only to eat and loaf."[12] Of course, not only Spanish hidalgos came for feudal riches in America; the early fiasco of English Jamestown illustrates the mentality of the "poore Gentlemen" who came to America to seek wealth without personal labor in America. Several of the middle and southern English American colonies were originally chartered as vast estates for peers (including a prince) of the realm, and even France at one point toyed with the idea of carving up the lands bordering the St. Lawrence as feudal estates. The early European settlers who came to the Americas were of that class of men who expected others to work for them, and the native Americans appeared to be a vast reservoir available to do that work.[13]

European colonists at first attempted to impress the natives they found as laborers, and large numbers of Indians were captured, traded, or sold by all Europeans—including the New England Puritans—for use on plantations in mainland and Caribbean colonies. But Indian labor generally proved to be unsuitable, since many of these slaves died, refused to work, or ran away. Although Indian slavery remained legal, it dwindled among the English and the French plantation owners as other kinds of exploitative labor were imported, first large numbers of indentured servants and ultimately the more satisfactory chattel slave labor of blacks from Africa.[14]

## SPANISH ENSLAVEMENT OF INDIANS

The Black Legend, however, fingered the Spanish as the greatest exploiters of Indian labor. The largest number of Indians fell within Spain's vast dominions and remained through at least the nineteenth century in various levels of exploitation.

Unlike the English, who removed their Indians from settled lands, Spain more visibly used those Indians who remained after the winnowing winds of disease had destroyed the majority of them. The sedentary Indians were used to fulfill multiple kinds of tributary and compulsory labor requirements—legally and illegally enforced—and the nomadic "wild" Indians were harvested by expeditions of slave hunters who carried them off to work in mines or to be raised as domestics, field hands, and guides or interpreters.

All the earliest Spanish explorers captured Indians in large numbers. By 1514 slaving expeditions were already probing the North American coast to find new labor to replace depleted Indian populations on plantations and in the mines of the Caribbean islands. Patents for exploration generally included provisions to distribute Indians among members of the expedition or to sell for the profit of the expedition. Ponce de León's 1513 expedition to Florida sought gold and slaves and was attacked in retaliation for earlier slave raids. By 1521 Spanish slavers were probing the Carolinas, and in 1539 Hernando de Soto took with him bloodhounds, chains, and iron collars for catching and keeping Indian slaves. Ironically, the first Europeans encountered in 1536 by Cabeza de Vaca on his trek back to Spanish civilization after having been enslaved himself for years by Indians of the Southwest was a large slave-hunting expedition whose leaders supplemented their already successful endeavor by enslaving de Vaca's friendly Indian escort as well.[15]

The forcible capture or maintenance of Indians was generally justified on the basis that it was a necessary process for civilization and Christianization and that Indian lives were better in captivity than in the poverty and uncertainty of barbaric nomadism or heathen idolatry—an argument almost identical to that which would be used later by the southern states in the nineteenth century to defend their practice of black slavery. Forcible Christianization was considered "the exercise of a just and pious doctrine against pagans and heathens,"[16] and those who practiced Indian slavery viewed it as the only "practicable method of civilizing and Christianizing wild Indians." "Half-animal beings," they needed to be "subjected to forced labor" and "be forced to learn productive labor." Unbaptized "wild" Indians had no rights.[17] Using both the justification of conquest and rebellion and the lofty goal of conversion of the heathen, the Spanish entered and claimed Indian lands and Indian souls. The military conquerors read to the

Indians—in unintelligible Spanish—Spain's claim to their land and labor in the name of king and church. The penalty for rebellion was war and its concomitant enslavement.

Yet, ironically, Spain had early developed one of the most enlightened body of laws of any European state to protect the Indians in its American provinces. Reformers such as Bartolomé de las Casas had influenced the crown to pass laws and create protectorates as early as 1516 to shield Indians from abuse. By 1526 chattel slavery had been forbidden by Spanish law; by the mid-1500s compulsory Indian labor in mines had been abolished and the fief-like *encomienda* forbidden, and by the late 1500s explicit Indian labor laws were being enacted.[18] Nevertheless, Spaniards, especially frontiersmen of all classes, continued to ignore the laws and exploit Christian and non-Christian Indians alike. *Encomiendas* were still worked and granted, slave raids into north-central Mexico and Chihuahua were active sources of captive Indian miners, and the seventeenth and eighteenth centuries were marked by slave raids on the Apachean tribes in New Mexico and Arizona.

The Spaniards who came to America were products of their country's culture, one foot still firmly planted in the feudal system and imbued with the remnants of the religious militancy that had fueled their crusades against the Muslims. In the Americas Spaniards were rewarded with "fiefs" in the form of *encomiendas* as their portion of the spoils of war. An *encomienda* was an allotment not of land but of the tribute labor of the Indian "serfs" within its boundaries and was awarded the *encomendero* for his and up to two generations of his heirs' lives. Tribute was exacted from the heads of families and collected by the *encomendero* for the crown and himself. In return for their *encomienda*, *encomenderos* were charged with the spiritual and temporal care and protection of those Indians entrusted to them and could be required to render military service when needed.[19] Despite the banning of the *encomienda* system in 1549, in order to pay for the colonization of New Mexico the crown allowed Juan de Oñate to grant up to thirty-five *encomiendas* following his *entrada* in 1598, and even promised one (though it was never awarded) to the *reconquistador*, Diego de Vargas, at the turn of the eighteenth century.[20]

As the number of Spaniards increased and the pool of Indian laborers decreased, the *encomienda* was replaced by corveé labor, the *repartimiento de indios*. Indian workers were coercively apportioned, in rotation, to Spanish employers who applied to government officials for them, and could be paid wages.

Ultimately, the systems of tribute labor were replaced by another kind of bondage, that of peonage or debt labor, which was epitomized in the classic hacienda tradition. Employers held their employees by keeping them in perpetual debt through loans that could be paid off only with labor, and these debts were inheritable by a peon's heirs, who also had to repay them with their labor.

## ENSLAVEMENT OF INDIANS IN NEW MEXICO

All the above-mentioned forms of institutional compulsory labor were used and abused in Spanish America, particularly on the frontiers, such as New Mexico, where inconvenient government policies were frequently ignored or winked at. Often there was little differentiation between *encomienda* tribute and *repartimiento* labor in Spanish colonies, and forced labor remained a part of the New Mexican tradition. From the early explorers who demanded food, shelter, clothing, and blankets from the Pueblo Indians, to later periods when the Indians were required to give tribute labor and goods to their Spanish overlords, the Spaniards in New Mexico expected native labor to provide for their support. Even mission Indians were virtual slaves to the demands of the missionaries, who needed them to work the fields and construct the mission buildings. Women who worked as domestics in Spanish homes were forced to put up with unwanted sexual advances as well.[21]

Such demands for labor contributed directly to several frontier uprisings by Indians, including the Indians of northern Mexico in 1602 and the Pueblo Revolt of 1680.[22] Although the system of tribute labor was reassessed after the Pueblo Revolt, the need for cheap labor remained and the enforcement of Indian labor continued to be the norm.

### ACQUISITION OF INDIAN SERVANTS

WARFARE

Spanish Americans continually found themselves short of workers, particularly on the frontier, and tribute labor from Christianized sedentary Indians came to be continually supplemented with captives taken from "wild" Indian bands. Such captives could not legally be taken solely for their use as slaves since Indian slavery was illegal, but there were many ways to get around this technicality. The capture of Indian slaves could be justified on the grounds of their having been taken in battle against hostile heathens. Thus these Indians became prisoners of war placed in servitude for a specified amount of time as punishment, and they also became suitable subjects for conversion to Christianity. In New Mexico the Apaches and Comanches were early targets of slave raiders looking for laborers for the mines of northern Mexico, but some were also distributed through the frontier settlements as domestics and field hands, especially young, trainable children. Along with the Apache and Comanches, numerous "Pawnee" captives also appeared in the records of the early 1700s, the result of several punitive expeditions onto the plains. Navajos and Utes became later targets.[23]

Captives were also purchased from nomadic tribes at annual trade fairs and or other trading rendezvous.[24] Generally, these captives were women and children captured as part of intertribal warfare and brought incidentally to the New Mexican trade fairs, where they were purchased "out" of their slavery by the Spaniards. As the market for captives became well known and established, however, intertribal warfare increased and became a means to the end of acquiring captives for sale.[25] Thus intertribal hostilities as well as warfare with the Indians by the Europeans themselves served a triple service for the Spaniards.

Not only did such slavery-induced, intertribal warfare keep the Spanish settlements supplied with labor and converts, but it also served, as a "special providence of God,"[26] to help sap the strength of potential enemies and direct their hostile energies elsewhere. To this end local officials and even the king of Spain encouraged the ransoming of Indian captives in order to save these children's lives and souls as well as to encourage alliances against enemy tribes or those allied with European enemies. Even José de Gálvez, *visitador general* to Mexico, noted as part of his 1767 solution to ongoing frontier Indian problems that "the vanquishment of the heathen consists in obliging them to destroy one another."[27] Nor were the Americans who later arrived in New Mexico slow to appreciate the same military potential, as New Mexican officials and politicians of the 1850s and 1860s also advocated the taking of captives as reparation for militia duty and to keep intertribal hostilities alive for the purpose of destroying enemy tribes.[28]

TRADE

The established practice of purchasing captives from Indians themselves had been ingrained through the old trade fair at Taos and later spread to other established rendezvous including the village of Abiquiú and sites in southeastern New Mexico.

So established was the trade at the annual fairs that the month in which it was held became known to some as the "month of slaves," and among the Comanches the month of September became known as the "Mexico Month" (September being the time when the harvest of slaves was taken to New Mexico). Annual Indian trading at Taos between the plains and Pueblo Indians predated the Spaniards, but with their arrival the annual trade became larger, richer, and more boisterous and brought more and more human trade goods.[29] Early Spanish chroniclers have described the fairs; Fr. Pedro Serrano depicted the New Mexican slave market in a graphic passage sent to the viceroy in 1761:

> It is the truth that when these barbarians bring a certain number of Indian women to sell among them many young maidens and girls, before delivering them to the Christians who buy them, if they are ten years old or over, they deflower and corrupt them in the sight of innumerable assemblies of barbarians and Catholics (neither more nor less as I say), without considering anything but their unbridled lust and brutal shamelessness and saying to those who buy them, with heathen impudence: "Now you can take her—now she is good."[30]

In 1776 Fr. Francisco Domínguez described the fair at Taos but was apparently less disturbed by the practice. Here the Indians

> bartered buffalo hides, "white elkskins," horses, mules, buffalo meat, [and] pagan Indians (of both sexes, children and adults) whom they capture from other nations. (In Father Claramonte's time Christians from other places *were also ransomed.* . . .)
>
> . . . [The rate of trade for] an Indian slave, [is] according to the individual, because if it is an Indian girl from twelve to twenty years old, two good horses and some trifles in addition. . . . If the slave is male, he is worth less and the amount is arranged in the manner described. (Emphasis added.)[31]

Of the fair at Abiquiú, where the southern Ute Indians came to trade, Domínguez wrote:

> Every year, between the end of October and the beginning of
> November, many heathens of the Ute nation come to the vicinity
> of this pueblo. They come very well laden with good deerskins,
> and they celebrate their fair with them. This is held for the sole
> purpose of buying horses [which are purchased for] fifteen to
> twenty good deerskins. . . . Sometimes there are little captive
> heathen Indians (male or female) as with the Comanches, whom
> they resemble in the manner of selling them.[32]

It didn't take long for the New Mexicans to find that they could acquire additional captives by going to the Indians as well as trading at the annual fairs. Residents of northern frontier settlements sought trade with the neighboring tribes, particularly the Utes. As knowledge of the trails north emerged through exploratory treks by men such as Juan de Rivera in 1765 and Fr. Francisco Domínguez and Fr. Silvestre Escalante in 1776, New Mexican traders ventured farther into the Ute country of Colorado and Utah. While Rivera traversed unknown territory in southwestern Colorado and as far as the Colorado River crossing at Moab, Utah, ten years later members of Domínguez's expedition would include experienced traders along the same trails.[33] Domínguez's trip opened the route across the Colorado into the land of the western Utes in Utah, and mountain men and other Mexican traders extended the route to Los Angeles, California. Capitalizing on this knowledge, New Mexican traders penetrated the interiors of Colorado and Utah in search of Indian trade, and by the turn of the nineteenth century Mexican traders annually traversed the Old Spanish Trail from Santa Fe, New Mexico, to central Utah and back. So predictable was the trade route, its timetable, and its preferred commodity that Indian "wholesalers" with children to barter anticipated the arrival of the traders and met them at convenient points along the way.[34]

After 1831 the trade extended into California. Beginning in the early spring, traders would carry inexpensive trade goods to barter with Navajos and Utes for worn-out horses.[35] These horses or mules were taken into Utah, where they were bartered, along with arms and ammunition, for Indian children and women who were carried into California and sold; more horses were purchased for the return trip to barter for more Indian women and children to be transported to New

*1. Santa Fé, New Mexico, 1859. Courtesy of the New Mexico Historical Society.*

Mexico. These seasonal caravans were often quite large, sometimes consisting of several hundred Mexican traders or as few as a dozen. So profitable was the commerce in captive children that a good trader could set himself up quite well after returning with only half a dozen Indian children to sell.[36]

As the trade increased, the Spanish government began to fear the flow of contraband, including arms, ammunition, and horses, to potentially hostile tribes on its border. Thus, between 1778 and 1824 Spanish officials attempted to interdict the trade by issuing regulations, first prohibiting unlicensed trade with the Indians and then forbidding outright the traffic in Indian captives. The frontier traders ignored or circumvented these laws, however, for the Indian trade provided too significant a portion of their income.[37] And it was not unusual for Indians themselves to bring their own children in for barter.

In addition to the trade fairs and caravans, New Mexicans acquired captives at rendezvous with Comanches and Apaches where they purchased not only Indian but Mexican captives from northern Mexico.[38] As Domínguez had noted in 1776, the attitude toward the purchase of Indian captives was that they were being ransomed or redeemed from their heathen captors. By maintaining this legal

1. OLD SPANISH TRAIL TO UTAH

fiction, New Mexicans could bypass the laws against the enslavement of Indians—or Mexicans—(Christian or not), and the church could sanction their "ransoming" for the purpose of temporal and especially spiritual salvation. In the tradition of classic Mexican peonage, then, the ransomed captive found himself in the role of an indebted servant who was required to work to pay off this debt, the cost of his redemption. As Domínguez noted in 1776, "a number of . . . Indians in this villa [Santa Fe] who after being *ransomed* from the pagans by our people are then emancipated to work out their account under them" (emphasis added).[39]

Small children made the best servants since they could be raised as acculturated, Catholic New Mexicans and be trained not only to do the work but to expect to do it.[40] According to one study, they were,

> in effect, held in a form of indentureship. The indentureship consisted of an unwritten agreement between the ransomer and colonial officials that the ransomed Indian would be free of obligation to the ransomer after she or he had provided services equal to their ransoms. The ransomer also agreed to instruct the Indian in Christianity and in the crafts, customs, and language of Spanish New Mexico. Some . . . did learn crafts while in this stage, but the majority were household servants or farm and ranch hands and complete economic dependents.[41]

## SLAVE RAIDS

It was only a short step from ransoming captives to acquiring them directly. Spaniards had been capturing hostile Indians since arriving in the New World; at the very least, some of the children of these hostile tribes, unsuitable for direct labor, found their way into the settlements alongside the regularly ransomed captives. New Mexicans soon began to incorporate slave raiding itself into their economy. But since this was strictly illegal, frontier slave hunters and their customers maintained the pretense of possessing only ransomed captives who were simply working off their debts.[42]

Continuing hostilities with the Indians provided a ready source of captives for the market for servants, and slave raids were guaranteed to keep such hostilities in force. In a vicious cycle New Mexicans would carry out raids against the Indians—Apache, Navajo, Comanche—taking herds and goods as well as human booty. In retaliation the Indians would raid the New Mexicans, stealing flocks, women, and children in return. Such retaliatory raids would spawn regular and irregular military responses in the form of attacks on the Indians, in which more booty and slaves would be taken as compensation by the "soldiers," which would initiate even more retaliatory raids by the Indians. The cycle would occasionally be broken by peace overtures from either side, but the New Mexicans' insatiable appetite for laborers would invariably launch new slave raids and begin the cycle again. So extensive was the slave raiding that when questioned in 1868 as to how many of his tribe were in captivity in New Mexico, Navajo chief Barboncito claimed, "Over half the tribe." One historian estimated that in 1865 New Mexicans held at least five to six thousand captive Navajos alone, and New Mexico Indian Superintendent Michael Steck estimated a minimum of two thousand. In 1868 Steck complained that the Indian slave trade was such a bad influence in the territory that "no permanent peace could be had with [the Indians] as long as this evil is permitted."[43]

Despite efforts by the United States to interdict the trade in order to effect peace, New Mexican slavers continued to ply their trade, often openly defying military officials and refusing to acknowledge peace treaties. When the Utah sources of captives dried up in the 1850s (following Pedro León Luján's trial and the passing of subsequent anti–Indian slavery laws), the confusion of the Civil War and the Navajo roundup and exodus to the Bosque Redondo turned New Mexicans increasingly to the Navajos. During the war against the Navajos and their subsequent roundup, large numbers of captives were taken, including friendlies trying to surrender or Indians who were caught away from the Bosque Redondo reservation. Although Kit Carson did not take slaves himself during the war, he openly advocated the allocation of Navajo captives as compensatory spoils of war for his Ute allies, but he was overridden by his superiors, who insisted that all prisoners be returned to Santa Fe and then sent to their reservation. Navajos came to dread "falling in with armed parties of citizens from whom they expect[ed] no mercy."[44]

Ultimately, U.S. officials more actively sought to end the slave trade; this effort, combined with the end of the Civil War and the relocation of Indians onto reservations, was a major factor in the decline of the New Mexican slave trade. Indians remained increasingly out of reach (although slavers were known to snatch captives who had strayed off reservations).[45]

Stopping the trade was difficult, however, since it was so deeply entrenched not only among the ordinary citizens—the average family had at least one Indian menial—but among officials as well. Owning Indian servants was a mark of prestige as well as wealth. For example, although illegal, in the mid-1600s Governor Luis de Rosas staffed his own workshops with Indian captives taken from trade with Plains Indians and raids on the Apaches and Utes.[46] And in 1761 Serrano noted that Indian slaves were the "gold and silver and the richest treasure for the governors, who gorge themselves first with the largest mouthfuls from the table [trade fairs] while the rest eat the crumbs."[47] Later Anglo-American officials were little different from their New Mexican predecessors, as Indian captives were owned not only by wealthy political figures but by Indian agents such as Kit Carson, Albert H. Pfeiffer, and Lafayette Head as well. In fact, most Mexican families who could afford it owned at least one Indian servant at one time or another.[48] Individuals were even known to launch their own raids to obtain personal servants, as did at least one bridegroom who went out Indian hunting in order to obtain servants for his new bride.[49] But the profitability of the trade was equally important in accounting for its persistence, for a trader in Indian captives could enrich himself with a single successful slave-raiding or trading expedition, with children bringing seventy-five to two hundred dollars in the 1850s and four hundred to five hundred dollars in the mid-1860s as reservations made Indian captives more scarce.[50]

### INTEGRATION OF INDIAN SERVANTS IN NEW MEXICO

### "RANSOMING" AND INDENTURING

The treatment and status of Indian menials in New Mexico was much more similar to that of an indentured servant than that of a slave. In the first place, they were, in theory, working to repay the cost of their redemption or ransom. Although many were the product of direct slave raids—even after Spain had abandoned making slaves of prisoners of war for specified amounts of time—the legal fiction of a ransom was maintained. Thus these Indians found themselves involuntarily enrolled in a system of debt bondage, but one, nevertheless, from which it was expected they would eventually be emancipated.

A look at the practice of indenturing in colonial British America demonstrates the similarity between the traditional Indian "slavery" practiced in New Mexico and indenturing.[51] As in New Mexico, some colonies such as Virginia had high demands for labor and found forced servitude to be one solution. In some ways, like the *encomienda* right to labor, indentures were contractual rights to an individual's labor, not the person himself. Generally, these contracts were sold to repay the cost of transportation to the American colonies—a contracted debt—and were an outgrowth of the English indenturing system in which a (usually) young person sold his or her services for specified amounts of time. Theoretically, these contracts were voluntary; on occasion, however, individuals were also shanghaied or kidnapped—or redeemed from prison—and taken to the Americas against their will, where contracts to their labor were sold at auction.

Until black slave labor largely replaced indenturing, indentured servitude was a major institution in colonial British America, forming the principal labor supply for many colonial settlements and a significant portion of early British immigration. For example, through the 1600s and 1700s such servants constituted nearly 75 percent of colonial immigration. Contracts were generally sold for five years, shorter than time allotted for Indian servants in New Mexico, although masters frequently extended them as punishment for various infractions of service rules. The treatment of indentured servants, though generally harsher than that of the more expensive slaves, was remarkably similar to that of slaves, except for the crucial difference that after their term of servitude, servants were free. Historian John Van Der Zee provides a description:

> They, the work they did, and the clothes on their backs belonged to their masters. They could be hired out, sold or auctioned, even if this meant separating them from their families. They could be beaten, whipped, or branded. If they ran away they could be punished by an extension, of a multiplicating of their term of servitude; in some colonies, runaways were hanged, a process too wasteful to apply to slaves, who retained, after all, the value of capital.[52]

Contracts to indentures could be sold at will by masters; some Virginia planters staked them as wagers in games of chance, and courts were even known to award "futures" in incoming indentures as court settlements. As historian Edmund Morgan puts it, "Virginians dealt in servants the way Englishmen dealt in land or chattels. . . . A servant, by going to Virginia, became for a number of years a thing, a commodity with a price." One angry English servant wrote, "My Master . . . hath sold me for a £150 sterling like a damned slave."[53]

The similarity between slavery and indenturing was not lost on these English servants. It was undoubtedly not lost on the less tutored Indian either. Like a slave or an English indentured servant, the Indian servant could be bought, sold, traded, or bartered during the term of servitude, or physically abused or exploited at his or her master's whim.

The concept of forced labor was, then, an inheritance for both the English and the Spanish Americas. Indenturing gave way to wage-earning servants as the labor pool increased in the North and black chattel slavery grew in the southern British-American colonies. But in Spanish America the concept of debt labor continued in the form of Indian slavery and debt peonage. Although the emancipation of the Indian "slave" was more likely than that of either the Mexican or Indian peon, peons could not (theoretically) be bought or sold like chattel as Indian captives could. The differentiation between chattel slaves and Indian servants or Mexican peons was highlighted even after the advent of an Anglo-American New Mexico when it was determined that neither Indian "slavery" nor peonage was covered by either the Emancipation Proclamation or the Thirteenth Amendment freeing black slaves: both forms of service were considered "voluntary" servitude, falling under the "Law Regulating Contracts between Masters and Servants" passed by Congress in 1858–59.[54]

TREATMENT AND FOSTERING

In New Mexico the treatment of Indian servants varied according to circumstances. Older captives, raised in their own culture, were more difficult to control and received harsher treatment, including frequent beatings or other abuse. Even small children sometimes suffered mistreatment, particularly during the earliest stages of captivity before they were situated with owners who would care for them. One Anglo observer wrote in 1852 that he had "seen frequently little children from 18 months to 6 years old, led around the country like beasts, by a Mexican who had probably stolen them from their mother not more than a week, and offered for sale for from 40 to 120 dollars."[55] Indeed, it was typically the slaver who most severely mistreated his prisoners. Once in a home, however, captive children were usually treated like one of the family.[56] All children in New Mexican homes worked at an early age and worked hard, and these adopted Indian children appear to have done work comparable to that of the other children in the home. All foster children—including both captive Indian children and the children of poorer relatives—tended to be worked a little harder.[57]

Physical abuse was more an exception than the rule for most Indian servants; more common was the abuse of extending the length of time required for service. Because Indian servants were without legal standing and without formal agreement as to the length of service required to pay back their "ransom," they were totally at the mercy of their owners. Nevertheless, servants who were abused could, by law, appeal to authorities—civil and ecclesiastical—for help and occasionally successfully did so.[58]

Children were generally adopted into the family of their masters, where they were fed, clothed, and educated into the survival skills of the frontier; raised in the Catholic religion; and given the family name. Theoretically, these servants were emancipated on reaching adulthood, between the ages of fifteen and twenty-one, or on their marriage, although it was not unknown for an unscrupulous owner to refuse to allow a servant to marry or to keep an unwitting servant in lifelong servitude. Likewise, even emancipated servants could be placed back into temporary servitude for "closer supervision" by civil authorities concerned about their behavior.[59]

Anxious to absolve himself as a dealer in slaves after his disastrous trial in Utah, Pedro León Luján had his friend Lafayette Head, later Ute Indian agent at Abiquiú, make a formal statement regarding the "buying and selling of Payutahs" and describing the New Mexican practice of "fostering" Indian children. According to Head:

> The parents gave the children [to León] but not for slaves—they are adopted into the family of those who get them, are baptized and remain & trusted as one of the family— The head of the house standing as Godfather. The Prefect has the right to free them whenever maltreated. The Indian has a right to choose a guardian— Women are freed whenever married—say from 14 to 16—Men ditto from 18 to 20— At the death of Godfather never sold—always freed.
>
> The Godfathers provide husbands and wives for them the same as their own children— . . . As soon as they are baptized they cannot be sold any more than the Mexican children—it would be contrary to the laws of the Church— They are no Peons—they have no debts to work out. They first learn to talk—then the Lords Prayer—then Baptized and adopted.
>
> There is no Mexican law on the subject—only custom.[60]

Although there are some inaccuracies in Head's statement—like any other indentured servant, Indians and even ransomed Mexicans could be bought and sold; godparents did not always find mates for their servants or fully emancipate them; and they were working to pay off their debt of ransom—his description was reasonably accurate regarding the integration of Indian children into the families and society. Another official noted in 1865 that whereas "some families abuse them, . . . others treat them like their own children."[61] Many Mexicans did look on their Indian children as adopted, and they frequently became trusted and even loved members of families, though often in the role of lesser kin.[62] In an 1833 court case in California, Antonio José Rocha testified that he had purchased an Indian boy from New Mexican traders "with the sole object of adopting the boy as a son and teaching him the principles of the Catholic religion; that when he should attain legal age he should be free."[63] And in 1867, when U.S. officials removed a Navajo boy from the home of a New Mexican, his owner complained, "I did not have the boy nor did I pretend to have him in captivity other than as an adopted son, whom I have raised as such. My family have regarded him as such and he has considered himself an equal member of the family."[64]

Indeed, during the late 1860s and early 1870s when U.S. officials were attempting to locate captive Indians to return to their own people as part of peace treaties and the attempt to stop the trade in Indian slaves, they found that not all the captives were willing to leave their New Mexican homes. Reluctantly, officials were forced to admit that there were merits to keeping many of the Indians in their current situations. Official reports gave examples of captives who "could not be induced to leave [their master's] service" and others who had "become much attached to the citizens."[65]

Other reports advised against returning a number of the captives to their tribes because acculturation was so complete as to make returning these individuals more damaging than allowing them to stay: they were baptized Catholics and had been raised as Hispanic New Mexicans; they were no longer "Indian." Another report remarked that "in some cases these people probably are better off by reason of their bondage, being secure of a home, than they would be otherwise," although "in by far the greater number of cases their plight cannot but excite our pity."[66] One Indian agent acknowledged the dilemma faced by officials trying to return captives in accordance with treaty promises, noting that "some [Indian children] living with the Mexicans are better situated than they would be with their parents [on the reservation]." Nevertheless, he recognized that the Indian parents also had "the same right to their children (that are under age) as any civilized people. They appear to have great love for their children, and treat them well."[67] One citizen wrote his belief that only

> one in fifty of them desire to leave their civilized life for a renewal
> of the barbarous and uncivilized life of their tribe. . . . It becomes
> then a serious question of humanity, whether those Navajos who
> are now voluntarily living among our people . . . shall be forced
> back upon savage life against their will . . . , or whether, by
> voluntary action they shall remain as they are, the objects of care
> by the church and civil protection by the Territory.[68]

## SOCIAL POSITION

During their years of "indentureship" Indian children learned the typical "peasant" skills of farming, herding, and domestic work of frontier New Mexico. Once they "repaid" their debt of redemption, they were emancipated. These detribalized, Christianized, and acculturated Indians, called *genízaros,*[69] entered free society on the lowest level, penniless and landless—and economically in competition with their former masters. Thus the majority chose to continue employment with former masters on wages or hired out to others, remaining in the farming-herding economy. Others engaged in crafts or trading or joined the military.[70]

In 1844 Josiah Gregg observed (rather ethnocentrically) that these captives who "resume their liberty intermarry with the race of their masters, becoming Mexican citizens, often undistinguishable from many of the already dark-hued natives."[71] Actually, marriage by Indian servants may have been discouraged by masters since it could equate with their servants' early emancipation. Sixty percent of captives were women, but only a small percentage of them seem to have married, although men were more likely to. Women did bear children, however; in one study of the baptismal records of Indian servants' children, nearly 75 percent were illegitimate. Some of the unknown fathers were probably the women's masters; many of the others were no doubt other Indian servants or *genízaros.*[72] Typically, *genízaros* tended to marry other *genízaros,* as well as occasionally, as one early writer put it, "with the lower class of Mexicans."[73]

*Genízaros* formed a definite social class, certainly not indistinguishable from other New Mexicans, as Gregg thought, but with, nevertheless, a social position that allowed them to function in the society and even to advance in it to some extent.[74] They formed a caste of dislocated, detribalized Christian Indians living under Spanish colonial authority.[75]

Integral to the *genízaro* economy was the military. All *genízaro* men originally supported or actively participated in profitable militia service against hostile Indians, which provided a continual source of income from war booty (the primary incentive for participating in Indian wars)—including the capture and sale of more Indian captives. *Genízaros* were considered ideal for this work because it was assumed they were more warlike and possessed knowledge of the Indian cultures they fought and the Indian territories they scouted. Many indeed had linguistic skills and were able to act as interpreters and scouts in their role of *indios exploradores*. As a result, *genízaros*—traditionally an economically deprived class—had access to good-paying government jobs and lucrative war booty. The military also afforded the *genízaro* a means for obtaining land. Land grants became available in return for required military service, and governors used *genízaros* to settle buffer communities on the Indian frontier borders such as Abiquiú or Cerro de Tomé. The *genízaros* were good Indian fighters, and they were expendable. But a frontier also offers leveling influences. Some *genízaros* were ultimately able, through increased wealth, land, and intermarriage, to achieve the tithe-paying *vecino* class of a respectable New Mexican, though this feat may have been more of an exception than the rule.[76]

Despite being respected for their loyal fighting, scouting, and interpretive abilities, however, *genízaros* were regarded by early chroniclers as lazy, vagabonds, "weak gamblers, liars, cheats, and petty thieves," a people without a viable political or economic organization, "fugitives" from their masters, and a generally "odious" people. As a label, the term *genízaro* came to and continues to be a derogatory epithet in New Mexico. The *genízaros* and their descendants were social inferiors, not as good as the true Spaniard, a descendant of servants, "a semi-slave, low class and without ability." Even today New Mexican Hispanics use the term to chastise misbehaving children.[77]

Nevertheless, these fostered and acculturated Indians found a distinct social niche in New Mexican society. It admittedly placed them in a socially inferior position, but economic opportunities were available through their military talents, and sufficient numbers of like *genízaros* existed for the formation of their own communities where they could marry and bear children.

After three hundred years the tradition of forced Indian servitude had become integral to New Mexican society. By the mid-nineteenth century thousands of Indian servants labored in an indentured debt bondage, the product of Indian warfare, trade, and slave raids, and ultimately formed a significant and distinct social caste in the territory. As a class these *genízaros* also came to perform needed services in New Mexico as valued and trusted members of the militia and settlers on dangerous Indian frontiers. Nevertheless, the tradition of obtaining slaves was a significant factor in maintaining Indian hostilities not only against the Spanish-Mexicans but against other Indian tribes as well, and the end of Indian hostilities and the end of Indian slaving went hand in hand. Undoubtedly, few of these servants would have chosen to be stolen from their homes, usually at the expense of the lives of their parents or relatives, carried about and mistreated by slavers, and disciplined by strange, new owners. But, once raised within the Hispanic culture, few desired to return to Indian ways, having become integrated and acculturated members of the Hispanic society themselves.

It was from such a cultural milieu that Pedro León Luján came. A product of frontier New Mexico and raised in a *genízaro* village steeped in the tradition of Indian trade, Don Pedro León was doubtless surprised and then confounded by the rigid antipathy shown by Utah Mormons toward his long-standing trade with the Utes. To him, his trade was not only profitable but customary and socially acceptable—and even in demand by both Indians and New Mexicans. The attitude of the Mormon judiciary into whose hands he fell must have at first disconcerted, then angered the old trader. He could not understand that the Utahns' experience with and perspective on the Indian slave trade was far different from his own.

## CHAPTER THREE

## THE INDIAN SLAVE TRADE IN UTAH

When Mormon pioneers entered Great Salt Lake Valley in 1847, they found a flourishing Indian slave trade between Utes and New Mexican traders along the Old Spanish Trail. They were dismayed by the practice, but not necessarily because they were abolitionists—some of the earliest pioneers were southern slave owners, and there were black slaves among the first settlers who entered the valley. However, Mormon ideology made a distinction between Negroes and American Indians; where forcible servitude was justifiable within Mormon doctrine for the black "sons of Cain," the American Indians were "Lamanites," a chosen remnant of the House of Israel on whom spiritual and priesthood blessings had been pronounced.

More important, though, the Mormons from the beginning regarded the slave trade as not only morally reprehensible but politically untenable as well. First, the Mormons found themselves in the center of the traditional Mexican/Indian slave route and saw only the uglier aspects of the operation: the cruelty of Indian slavers toward their merchandise. Almost as bad, the fate of these slaves was to be purchased by Mexicans, who, in the eyes of the Mormons, with their nineteenth-century prejudice, were little better than the Indians themselves. The Indian slavers also tried to foist their excess merchandise onto the Mormon newcomers, usually at a price higher than the reluctant purchaser could afford to pay.

Perhaps of even more importance, the slave trade itself threatened the peaceful settlement of the Mormons' promised land. Slave raiding by Utes stirred up hostility and fear among the tribes they warred with or preyed on. The Mormons found themselves caught between the warring tribes, each of which they needed as a peaceful ally in order to settle safely in their far-flung colonies, yet each making demands on its alliance. To worsen matters, the Mexican trade helped sustain these conflicts with its traffic in arms, ammunition, and horses.

Yet despite their abhorrence of the Indian slave trade, within weeks of their entrance into the Great Salt Lake Valley the new Mormon settlers were forced to become a party to it. Although they never actively sought Indian servants simply for the purpose of acquiring menials as the Spanish and Mexicans did, Mormons began to purchase Indian children from slavers as well as directly from destitute Indian families. Within a few years they would legalize and institutionalize this practice, justifying it—as the Spanish had already done—through the need for temporal and spiritual redemption of the Indian. Terminology was managed, and in an already familiar pattern in New Mexico, the practice of purchasing Indian children became not slavery but ransoming into an indenture. Purchase became a form of manumission, the cost of which would be repaid by the indentured Indian through service to his or her purchaser.

## MORMON ATTITUDES TOWARD BLACKS AND SLAVERY

The early Mormon church membership was drawn predominantly from the free North: Ohio and upstate New York, where it was born. Thus, the general attitude of church members toward slavery was negative, and most would originally have qualified as abolitionists or, at the least, Free-Soilers. When Mormon settlers moved to Missouri in the 1830s, they found themselves at odds with their non-Mormon neighbors, who were slaveholders or had come from southern slave states. Indeed, it was partly the concern over the growing number of Free-Soil Mormons, the question of blacks in the church, and the fear that free Negroes would immigrate into Missouri that helped spark the first riots and mob action against the Mormons in Independence, Missouri.[1]

In response to the need for peaceful integration of the abolitionist Mormons within this slave state (not to mention the desire for converts among southerners), the leadership of the young church reevaluated its position on slavery and blacks. The result was a conciliatory stance *against* abolition and the banning of abolitionist rhetoric from formal discourses. Some leaders attempted to explain the existence of black slavery by turning to Scripture, which decreed that the descendants of Cain (usually identified as Negroes) should always be servants.[2]

Slaves traveled west with the vanguard of the Mormon pioneers in 1847 when southern owners joined the trek to Utah. One man even gave one of his slaves, Green Flake, to Brigham Young as a teamster, and it was he, according to family tradition, who drove the carriage in which Brigham Young was riding when he entered the valley of the Great Salt Lake. Thus, black slavery arrived in Utah with the first Mormons.[3] By 1850, however, the majority of blacks in Utah were free (including Green Flake and other blacks given as tithing and in Young's service), except for twenty-six who were listed as being on their way to California with their masters, all but one of whom were from southern slave states.[4]

The political turmoil that surrounded the application of "Deseret" for statehood in 1849–50 was heavily influenced by the ongoing debate between the northern and southern states over slavery and the balance of power between the North and South. Southern states opposed the new state, fearing it would enter as "free" (though some northern states simply opposed a Mormon state). The request for statehood was disallowed in favor of organizing the Mormon domain as a territory. The 1850 compromise measure passed by Congress allowed the new Utah and New Mexico territories the right to choose whether to enter the Union as free or slave, though it was generally expected that both would be free.[5] Ironically, the Pedro León court case forced Utah to examine its own stand on the question of slavery, which it ultimately determined was legal; within a month the territorial legislature would pass laws regulating black slavery—specifically, the treatment of slaves—until its abolition in 1865. As a result, Utah became the only slave territory in the Far West.[6]

And yet the judicial and legislative recognition of slavery did not reflect the attitude of the majority of the people or their leaders. Brigham Young addressed the legislature in early January 1852, following the conviction of Luján and company and the determination of the court that black slavery was legal. Giving his personal opinion on the matter of slavery, he said, "It is unnecessary perhaps for me to indicate the true policy for Utah in regard to slavery. Restrictions of law and government make all servants; but human flesh to be dealt in as property, is not consistent or compatible with the true principles of government. My own feelings are that no property can or should be recognized as existing in slaves, either Indian or African."[7]

Nevertheless, black slavery remained legal. Still, the number of slave owners in Utah between 1847 and 1865 was very small, almost exclusively families that had grown up in the South and had brought their slaves west with them (in many cases, slaves who came willingly). The vast majority of the Mormons deplored slavery, acknowledging its legality only grudgingly.[8]

Mormons did not recognize the right of Indian slavery at all and were deeply shocked at the cruelty exhibited by Indian slavers to their captives. Thus the legislature legalized the indenturing and manumission of Indians in order to retrieve them from the hands of slavers, at the same time allowing the continuing ownership of black slaves.

## MORMON ATTITUDES TOWARD INDIANS

The official Mormon attitude toward the American Indian was vastly different from the American norm. The Mormon scripture, *The Book of Mormon,* purported to be a religious history of the ancestors of the American Indian; these Indians, known as "Lamanites," were regarded as the "fallen" descendants of the House of Israel—a refuge branch that had broken off and fled Jerusalem at the time of the Babylonian conquest—and entitled to the birthright blessings due the descendants of the biblical patriarch, Abraham. It was the responsibility of the Mormons to redeem the Indians, both physically and spiritually, so that they would become a white (or fair), "delightsome," and industrious people, worthy to receive those blessings.[9] A prominent Mormon preached that "the Lord has caused us to come here [Utah] for this very purpose, that we might accomplish the redemption of these suffering degraded Israelites. . . . It is a great privilege indeed . . . that we enjoy being associated with them in the accomplishment of so great a work."[10]

Therefore, unlike common Anglo or Hispanic attitudes toward Indians, in the Mormon view Indians were not (at least in theory) to be exploited, destroyed, or ignored. Mormons felt that part of their religious duty included caring about and for Indians; their scriptures prophesied of these Indian descendants that one day the gentiles should "bring thy sons in their arms, and [carry] thy daughters . . . upon their shoulders."[11] It is not surprising, then, that the first Mormon settlers were appalled at the cruel practices of the Indian slave trade in Utah.

## THE INDIAN SLAVE TRADE

The ongoing market for Indian servants in New Mexico had bred an active trade in captives along the Old Spanish Trail in Utah. These children came from several sources: some were purchased directly from families, some were the captives of more powerful bands of Indians (such as the Utes) who had learned to prey on weaker tribes, and occasionally some were taken captive by the Mexicans themselves.

Fortunes were to be made by the enterprising Mexican or Indian who grasped the opportunities to be found along the trail. Several Utah chiefs acquired great wealth and renown based on their slaving and horse-raiding activities. Wákara

*2. Wákara and Arapeen, Ute war chiefs and slave traders. Courtesy of the Utah State Historical Society.*

(also known as "Walker" or "Devil Walker" by the Mormons),[12] most prominent and shrewd of these Ute raiders, arrogantly ranged throughout Utah south of "Point of the Mountain," which separated the Salt Lake and Utah valleys, the Shoshone and Ute territories, respectively. He referred to central and southern Utah as "his country" and, with his heavily armed and mounted warriors, controlled and tolled the trade on the Old Spanish Trail. John C. Frémont remembered meeting him and his entourage in 1844, "journeying slowly towards the Spanish Trail to levy their usual tribute upon the great California caravans. . . . They conducted their depredations with form and under the color of trade and toll for passing through their country."[13]

Wákara was also the scourge of the weaker "Piede" Indians and was seldom seen without captive children to trade.[14] His desire to have a ready market for captives nearby may have prompted his invitation to Mormon leaders to settle in his home territories, leading to the establishment of Manti (a hundred and thirty miles south of Great Salt Lake City in Sanpete Valley) and Parowan (a hundred and eighty miles south of Great Salt Lake City on the southern California trail), which were central locations for his trading rendezvous.[15]

The sources of these captives were the weaker, pedestrian tribes such as the Paiute and Gosiute "Digger" Indians. For these tribes, the selling of children was sometimes a means of simple survival. Some parents sold their children because food was so scarce that they were sure to starve if their parents kept them. These Utah and Nevada desert Indians were so poor they often subsisted on whatever food they could find, including grubs, ants, grasshoppers, lizards, and snails, and had even been known to resort to cannibalism. Their clothing was practically nonexistent, and their shelters were brush enclosures or even holes in the ground. Following harsh winters they might be seen foraging among the frozen remains of their families, eating only grass. Early chroniclers described them as "degraded," "depraved," "least intellectual," and "*les Dignes de pitié*" (the people deserving of pity).[16] Hopi traditions recall Paiutes trading children for food at their pueblos,[17] and they were known to offer them to Mexican and Ute traders and later to the Mormon settlers, too. There are even reports that in order to stave off starvation in times of great stress these impoverished Indians may have eaten human flesh, perhaps even that of their own children.[18]

By the mid-nineteenth century Paiute women and children had become fearful of any mounted strangers. At the approach of such riders Paiute women would take their children to hide—often snatching them up while on the run by a looped belt kept around the child for that purpose—fearing both the raider and the trader, for even their own husbands could be tempted to barter them away for the price of a horse or a gun.[19] As one old Paiute explained, "They could make more children but they had nothing else to trade for horses and guns."[20] So frequently were these poor

*3. Paiute dwellings, 1850. John K. Hillers photograph, 1873. Courtesy of the Smithsonian Institution.*

Indians raided or traded, that they were in danger of dwindling into extinction, as it was their child-bearing women and children who were lost to them. Garland Hurt, Utah Indian agent in 1860, reported that "scarcely one-half of the Pyeed children are permitted to grow up in the band; and, a large majority of those being males, this and other causes are tending to depopulate their bands very rapidly."[21]

When the Mormon settlers entered the region, they did not seek the Indian slave trade but quickly found it thrust on them. Within weeks of arriving in the valley of the Great Salt Lake they were approached by an Indian named Baptiste,

4. *Paiute Indian children. John K. Hillers photograph, 1873. Courtesy of the Smithsonian Institution.*

who offered two teen-aged captives for sale. This is not surprising, since the Indians had been selling captives to Mexicans and mountain men for decades. But the new settlers were not interested in purchasing any Indians, even though Baptiste threatened to kill his captives if they didn't. After he carried out his threat by killing one, Brigham Young's son-in-law, Charles Decker, purchased the second for a gun. She was taken and raised in Brigham Young's home, where, according to Young, she "fared as [his] children, and [was] as free."²²

In another incident that summer two other small children captured in a battle with Shoshones were being tortured to death when Mormons sought to intervene. The seven-year-old daughter of a prominent chief was still alive but, wrote John R. Young, had been turned into "the saddest looking piece of humanity I have ever seen. They had shingled her head with butcher knives and fire brands. All the fleshy parts of her body, legs and arms had been hacked with knives, then fire brands had been stuck into the wounds. She was gaunt with hunger and smeared from head to foot with blood and ashes."[23] She was also purchased by Charles Decker, given to Brigham Young, and raised with his other children.[24] On another occasion Wákara's kin brother, Arapeen, offered several children for sale to settlers in Utah Valley.[25] When his offer was refused, he grabbed a child by the heels and smashed its head on the hard ground. After throwing the lifeless body at the feet of the horrified Mormons, he blamed them for the child's death, saying they "had no hearts, or [they] would have bought it and saved its life."[26]

Such coercive salesmanship was not unusual for the Utes. As early as 1813 a Mexican party of enterprising fur traders under the leadership of Mauricio Arze and Lagos García returned to New Mexico with a similar tale of the forcible sale of captives. Although the Spaniards were apparently seeking to trade for furs, the Timpanogos Utes (*tipana'núu-ci*) in Utah Valley wanted to trade horses for children instead. When they were refused, the angry Indians slaughtered a number of the traders' horses; after another hostile encounter with Sanpitch Indians the Spaniards cut their trek short and headed home. On the Green River they met another chief (Guasache) waiting, "as was his custom," for traders with whom he could barter. When he, too, demanded horses for children, the traders acquiesced, fearful of another attack similar to that of the Timpanogos Utes.[27]

Apparently, the Utes had long practice in selling their captives to willing or unwilling traders. Thus the entrance of the Mormons into Ute territory may have at first have seemed like the market coming to the seller. The Mormons' initial reluctance to purchase Indian captives posed no real problem for the Indian slavers. To make a sale Wákara needed only to threaten to sell them to Mexican slavers or Navajos (another active market for domestics and herders) or to kill them.[28] Brigham Young testified:

> Indian Walker has been in the habit for years in trafficking in
> Indians. He has never been here with his band without having a
> quantity of Indian Children as slaves—he offers them for sale, and
> when he has an offer that satisfies him in the price, he sells them,
> and when he cannot get what he thinks they are worth, he says he

will take them to the Navahoe Indians, or Spaniards, and sell
them, or kill them which he frequently does.[29]

The abusive treatment of the Indian captives was an added incentive to the
Mormon settlers to attempt to redeem the children and save them from further
cruelty or even death. Young testified, "I have seen Walkers slaves so emaciated
they were not able to stand upon their feet. He is in the habit of tying them out
from their camps at night, naked and destitute of food, unless it is so cold he
apprehends they will freeze to death. In that case he will give them something to
sleep on, lest he should lose them."[30] And the Utah legislature noted:

> It is a well established fact that women and children thus
> obtained, or obtained by war, or theft, or in any other manner, are
> by them frequently carried from place to place packed upon
> horses or mules; larietted out to subsist upon grass, roots, or
> starve; and are frequently bound with thongs made of rawhide,
> until their hands and feet become swollen, mutilated, inflamed
> with pain and wounded, and, when with suffering, cold, hunger
> and abuse they fall sick so as to become troublesome, are
> frequently slain by their masters to get rid of them. . . .
>
> . . . They do frequently kill their women and children taken
> prisoners, either for revenge, or for amusement, or through the
> influence of tradition, unless they are tempted to exchange them
> for trade, which they usually do if they have an opportunity. . . .
>
> . . . When the inhabitants do not purchase or trade for those so
> offered for sale, they are generally doomed to the most miserable
> existence, suffering the tortures of every species of cruelty, until
> death kindly relieves them.[31]

Because the Mormons saw the physical redemption and spiritual salvation of the
Indian as part of their religious and humanitarian responsibilities, the Indian slave
trade may have seemed particularly reprehensible to them. Utah leaders recognized
early that there was more than just the occasional incident of slave trading; they
knew that the annual trade with the Mexicans was a firmly established tradition

and a major factor in creating the market that encouraged the practice.[32] But at this point there was little the Mormons could do to stop the trade cold. The Utes had captives they insisted on selling to both Mormons and Mexicans, while the more destitute Indians continued to approach the settlers to sell their own children.

The potential for acquiring dislocated Indian children who could be raised and acculturated within the Mormon culture and religion was also a significant factor. This motivation may account for the number of Indian children who were purchased by Mormons without coercion or directly from Paiute parents themselves. George A. Smith, a prominent Mormon official and one of the attorneys of record defending Luján, remembered in his diary the Mormon trade in Indian children. In December 1850, while he was leading an expedition of settlers into southwestern Utah, a couple of his oxen were shot by Indians. After finding the guilty Indians half-naked and half-starved in the subzero weather, Smith

> told [the Indian] it was too late to cry, but if he would let me have the boy he might have the ox, to which he readily agreed. I told him the boy should be well-fed, comfortably clothed and made a man of if he would be a good boy. The Indian said he wanted to see him dressed like a white man, on his return. I told Mr. Empy he could take the boy for the present and take care of him. The Indian pointing to Br. Empy told the boy that was his father. The boy immediately followed Br. Empy seeming much pleased. Br. Empy took off his clothes and gave them to the Indian, and clothed him in his presence and gave the old Indian a shirt.[33]

Smith's experience with this "adoption" was not unusual. One traveler in 1853 noted that the Paiute children purchased by southern Utah families were taught to call their "protectors 'father' and 'mother,'" and that although the children were not kept from seeing their own people, who frequently came to their towns, "the latter evince very little interest in their offspring, for, having sold them to the whites, they no longer consider them their kith and kin."[34]

Others dealt directly with the Indian traders voluntarily. On more than one occasion G. A. Smith acted as intermediary between settlers and Indian traders. For example, in March 1851 he recorded an incident in which a Br. Bernard had traded a cow and a shirt to Wákara for a four-year-old Paiute girl, but the Ute leader was dissatisfied with the trade, wanting an ox instead. Smith advised Bernard to return the girl. A week later, however, Bernard presented Smith with a four-year-old "Pihede" girl "purchased . . . off Walker for an ox." A few days later an express from Great Salt Lake City remarked on Bernard, who was then in possession of another two Indian children purchased from Wákara and "lashed on a mule."[35]

Brigham Young may have taken his first step toward stopping the Mexican-Indian slave trade in the spring of 1851. Perhaps to circumvent the Mexican traders—as well as to proselytize the Indians—Young publicly advised members of his church to "buy up the Lamanite children as fast as they could, and educate them and teach them the gospel."[36] It may well be that this was a first tentative attempt to fight the Mexican trade by absorbing the captives before the Mexican traders had a chance to purchase them themselves; perhaps the Mormons hoped that if the merchandise was unavailable the trade would eventually end. The annual fall trek into central Utah by Mexican traders led by Don Pedro León brought the situation to a head, however, providing Utah officials with the incident and legal precedents they needed to fight the trade openly on the necessary two levels: interdiction of the trade and absorption of local captives.

The first step was to curtail the commerce by cutting off immediate access to the Mexican market; as the new ex officio superintendent of Indian affairs for the recently created Utah Territory, Brigham Young now had the power to grant or deny applications for trade with Indians within his jurisdiction under the Trade and Intercourse Act. Preventing trade between Mexicans and Indians in Utah Territory would go a long way toward solving the problem of the slave market as well as the uncontrolled sale of arms to the Indians. That left the Indian suppliers, who would still be trying to sell their captives; with one outlet closed, the Mormon market would become more important—and the Utes had already given the settlers adequate demonstration of what they were capable of doing to their unsold merchandise. Thus, while disallowing the sale of Indian captives (to outsiders), the Utah settlers still needed a mechanism whereby they could purchase these children and women, who would otherwise be abused or killed by their captors.

The trial of Pedro León et al. would provide the Utah courts and legislature the mechanisms by which the legal precedents could be set and new laws enacted that could accomplish all these goals.

## CHAPTER FOUR

## PEDRO LEÓN LUJÁN

The excoriated Pedro León of Utah history books was actually Pedro León Luján, a moderately well-to-do and respected citizen of Abiquiú, New Mexico. Don Pedro León—Pedro León on his trade license and in the Utah courts or Pedro León Luján, military commander, Indian trader, and local farmer in New Mexico—was a difficult man to pin down in New Mexico records.

Christening records (1754–1866) and census records reveal that there were no Leóns in Abiquiú or the surrounding area in the mid-1800s, and a review of other similar records throughout northern New Mexico show that the León surname was rare there. Military and Indian agency records, however, do reveal the presence in Abiquiú of a veteran of the Navajo and Apache Indian wars and an established trader among the Ute Indians by the name of Pedro León Luján. There is little doubt that this was the man who stumbled into the spotlight of Utah history while attending to his long-standing trade business among the central Utah Utes in Sanpete Valley.

Pedro León Luján was born in Abiquiú on April 8, 1794, the son of Juan Antonio Luján and María Ysadora Romero (widow of José Antonio Chávez), both long-time residents of that *genízaro* village. At least two other children, a son and a daughter, had been born to the couple before Pedro León's birth. Pedro León Luján was married at least three times, although Abiquiú records reveal only one child ever having been born to him, a son, José Agapito, christened in 1828. But records also disclose at least four Ute or Paiute Indian servants christened under his aegis or living in his home, and other children, possibly offspring of his second and third wives, lived there as well. Luján's first wife was María Manuela García (md. 1826), although census records later indicate that Luján lived with a Doña Juana Jaramío (1845) and an Anamaría (1850–70).[1]

To understand this man, Pedro León Luján, it is necessary to understand the milieu from which he came, particularly the home and culture in which he was raised. Luján's home was the village of Abiquiú, originally settled by *genízaros*, the detribalized and acculturated Indians who were either former Indian captives or Hispanicized Pueblo Indians unwelcome in their own pueblos. *Genízaros* from Santa Fe were sent as early as the 1740s to establish the village as a frontier buffer settlement with its own Catholic mission and the idealistic vision of helping "reduce" the nomadic tribes in the north to a sedentary Christian lifestyle.

The original village was located on a hill overlooking the Chama River valley, near the site of a long-abandoned Indian pueblo and chosen with an eye to its necessarily defensive position. In its early years the settlement was plagued with a series of disastrous confrontations with the Indians—Utes and Jicarilla Apaches—on whose borders it lay. The village was abandoned and forcibly resettled on the governor's orders several times, the last resettlement as late as 1770. The *genízaros* were eventually joined by Hispanic settlers, who established small plazas and outlying farms or ranches along the Chama River below the original settlement. Ultimately, the entire general region, with a dominant population of Hispanics, would be regarded as Abiquiú; for a long time, however, the village of Abiquiú proper would remain predominantly *genízaro*.[2] For this reason, it is very possible that Luján's family, noted in church records as being *vecinos* (tithe-paying settler-citizens) of the village of Abiquiú itself, had *genízaro* roots, with intermarriage and improved economic status bringing in the Spanish bloodlines or wealth that entitled them to the designation *españols* by the late eighteenth century.[3]

In its position on the New Mexican frontier, Abiquiú became a valuable buffer zone between nomadic Indians and the sedentary Hispanic settlements. It also hosted fall trade fairs with the Utes, served as an outfitting station for military expeditions against the Navajos, and was the last point of departure for traders and explorers traveling north along what would become the Old Spanish Trail. Later it would be the site of treaty negotiations between the United States and the Southern Ute bands, as well as a distribution center for rations and a short-lived Indian agency. During the rush for precious minerals in the San Juan Mountains in the 1860s and 1870s, Abiquiú would serve as a provisioning point for miners and facilitate the eventual expansion of the New Mexican frontier north and west along the San Juan River by Chama River valley residents. Abiquiú was particularly noted as a rendezvous for trade with the Ute Indians, both legal and illegal (since Indian trade had been banned by Spanish government proclamations for much of New Spain's history), and, most important for the

5. *San Tomás church and center of the village of Abiquiú, New Mexico. Courtesy of the New Mexico Historical Society.*

history of Luján, was one of three major centers of the illicit Indian slave trade in northwest New Mexico.[4]

Luján's father, Juan Antonio Luján, was listed as a "child of the Pueblo" in his marriage record and was likely of *genízaro* background. His mother was listed as a *vecina* and may have been of either Spanish or mestizo blood.[5] As the widow of José Antonio Chávez, she may have given Don Pedro León a step-relationship to the prominent Chávez family of Abiquiú. Luján's contemporary, José María Chávez, would serve as a mounted militia officer (ranking as high as a brigadier general) during wars against the Navajos and Apaches and would pick Luján as one of his four militia captains in the Apache campaign of 1854. Apparently, he also made at least one attempt at investing in the Indian trade: the year before Luján's abortive expedition into Utah, Chávez was issued a license to trade with the Utes in Utah Territory. Chávez is still remembered in Abiquiú as not only a prominent early citizen but one of the wealthiest as well.[6]

*6. Looking north up Chama Valley from Abiquiú: the beginning of the Old Spanish Trail. Courtesy of the New Mexico Historical Society.*

It has been argued by some historians that the New Mexican and Arizona Indian wars were fueled and perpetuated by slave profiteers, who used the hostilities as an excuse to raid Indians in order to "harvest" slaves; local militias, particularly from the three major slaving rendezvous of Cebolleta, Cubero, and Abiquiú, were eager volunteers in these actions. In some cases, these volunteers may have been instrumental in initiating the very wars they volunteered to participate in.[7] It is, then, significant that Luján was an active and conspicuous member of the Abiquiú militia.

Luján was prominent in records of major militia campaigns during the Mexican and U.S. territorial periods, and he may have participated in a number of unrecorded militia operations. He first appears in official Mexican records in 1836 on the Abiquiú militia muster rolls for that year's Navajo campaign.[8] By 1839 he had risen from a simple militiaman to a position of military leadership. In December of that year he submitted to the governor a report of militia troop strength from Abiquiú for a Navajo campaign, followed by a report on the official sortie against those Indians, which he led the same month. In that campaign Captain Don Pedro León Luján's troops attacked a small "ranchería," where they killed two warriors and a woman and captured "six little slaves of both sexes" along with considerable other plunder.[9]

Luján continued to achieve a reputation as a Mexican of social prominence—or at least influence—as well as an Indian fighter. Two years after the 1839 campaign

Luján wrote to Mexican officials that Navajo messengers sent by Chief Cayetanito had come to him at his home in Abiquiú to report that the tribe was gathered on the Río Puerco and wished him to help arrange peace talks with Mexican officials.[10]

In the summer of 1854, two years after his trial in Utah, Luján was one of four officers under the command of Brigadier General José María Chávez who captained brigades of more than two hundred mounted militiamen in a six-month campaign against the Jicarilla Apaches in northern New Mexico. Called into service by William Meservy, acting governor of New Mexico, in May 1854, the Abiquiú militia served both in the field and on call until discharged in August of that year. Luján saw action in the Sierra de los Gallinas and Sierra de Canjilón in pursuit of Indians who had raided Mexican settlements. Apparently, members of the militia were not compensated by the U.S. government as per agreements, and the officers were forced to press their claims in court for six years before receiving compensation for salaries and equipment.[11]

Because of Luján's experience as a member of the Abiquiú militia, we would expect his name to appear as a participant in the Ute campaigns of 1845 and 1846, in which the Abiquiú militia took an active part. And yet, although Chávez was an officer in these campaigns, it is significant that there is no record of Luján as part of his village's militia, despite his also having been prominent in the Indian wars both before and after the Ute operations.[12] If his relationship with the Utes as a long-accepted and well-known trader is taken into account, however, it is less surprising that a man who may have made a substantial portion of his income from trading with the Utes would not have wished to participate in campaigns against them. By remaining aloof from these military actions—especially in a leadership position—Luján could have preserved his trading relationships as well as travel immunity through Ute country along the Old Spanish Trail.

There is no question that Luján was a long-time trader among the Utes of southern Colorado, where he probably traded for the buckskins they were renowned for, as well as in central Utah, where he acquired Indian children to sell as servants in New Mexico. Luján had been trading for years among the central Utah Utes for their children before the Mormon hegira to the Wasatch front put a stop to that particular enterprise. According to Luján's Manti attorney, Andrew Siler, the Ute chief Arapeen "says that Pedro León has been trading with him for years, and Siapand an Indian who is here says that Pedro León traded with Arapine's father years ago."[13] Luján had christened at least two Ute Indian servant boys in 1833 and 1840; and in 1870 Luján had two Paiute (Pah Ute) boys living in his household, eleven and fourteen years of age, who had to have been acquired no earlier than 1857 and possibly as late as 1860—five to eight years *after* Mexican traders had been banned from Utah.[14] And as late as July 1864 Luján was apparently still trading at least among Utes of southern Colorado, for he reported witnessing Ute agitation in Colorado Territory to the New Mexico Indian Superintendency. Luján had just returned from the Weeminuche Ute country (probably around Cortez, Colorado), where the Tabeguache band had "invited them to join them in a war against the people of Conejos."[15]

It is also clear from government census records that Luján, although illiterate, was a man of moderate substance. Although he could not have been classed as wealthy, his farm holdings were valued at nearly three to four times that of the average farmer in the area: for example, in 1850 his real estate was worth more than one thousand dollars, whereas most surrounding farms were listed at two to three hundred dollars. Certainly Luján had sufficient resources to post the required one-thousand-dollar bond when he applied for a license for his ill-fated trading expedition of 1851.[16]

Thus we have in Pedro León Luján a moderately successful and solid citizen of frontier New Mexico, recognized by Indians, New Mexicans, and Americans as being a skilled military leader and Indian trader. He was obviously independent and proud; his militia experience points to his having an upper-class status inasmuch as he holds leadership positions and is referred to in military and census records as *Don* Pedro León, a title of prestige. He was also an experienced leader of trading expeditions in which others worked for him. Moreover, Luján was not afraid to tackle the American judicial system and bureaucracy, as evidenced by his legal attempts at redress in both Utah and New Mexico following his conviction in Great Salt Lake City and his joining in a suit against the U.S. government to recover back pay and compensation for his and his men's militia activity against the Apaches. We also find a man raised on the frontier of New Mexico, where trading with the Utes and other Indians was part of the normal economy and where the trade in captive Indian children was commonplace. We see the old trader still active at the age of seventy traveling among the southern Utes of Colorado and still dealing in—or at least owning—Utah Indian captives as he neared his eightieth birthday.

The veteran trader was an experienced fifty-seven years old when he organized one of his last open expeditions in 1851 to trade with the Utes of southern Colorado and the slaving Utes of central Utah.

## CHAPTER FIVE

## THE TRIAL OF DON PEDRO LEÓN

In November 1851 Utah officials found the incident they needed to bring the question of Indian slavery and Mexican trade to a head. "Spanish" traders from New Mexico,[1] including their leader, Pedro León Luján, were caught with Indian captives in their possession after they had been specifically refused a license to trade with the Indians. This prima facie evidence of their guilt brought them to court in Manti and then again in the First District Court of Utah Territory in Great Salt Lake City.

The main issue of the trial was the traffic in Indian slaves, which the Utah officials wished to stop. Because slavery itself was not illegal in Utah, the Mexicans could not be tried simply for having slaves in their possession. Their moral and political offense was possessing *Indian* slaves, although the legality of this charge was murky since there was no clear precedent concerning the legality of owning Indian slaves; Negroes could be enslaved, so why couldn't Indians? Consequently, the Mexicans were accused and tried for the only regulatory laws that they had actually violated: the laws regulating the trade and traffic with Indian tribes, found in the Trade and Intercourse Act of 1834, which had just been extended over Utah Territory in 1851.

The four-day trial forced official evaluation of slavery in general and Indian slavery in particular. The court had to examine the definition of "Indian country" and the control of trade within it as it related to the colonization of Utah Territory. The trial also helped crystallize formal legislative policies concerning both black slavery and the Indian slave trade, in which, though they found it repugnant, Utah citizens found themselves active participants.

### THE INCIDENT

The year 1851 found the Mormons beginning to expand southward into the strongholds of the warrior Utes. Provo had been established in 1849 in the midst of prime Ute settlements along Utah Lake, and a new settlement, Manti, had just been made eighty miles south in Sanpete Valley. Here were the two major concentrations of Ute activity, one a center for rendezvousing with trade caravans from New Mexico.

But the Indian slave trade impinged on this southern thrust of Mormon settlements. Thus, Utah officials saw the ending of the slave trade and the expulsion of New Mexican slave traders from the territorial boundaries of Utah as a high priority. Such a move would protect the Mormons' increasingly far-flung settlements, bring the Indians within the territory more closely under their control, and help hasten the civilization and (Mormon) Christianization of those same Indians.

Meanwhile, the U.S. Congress was beginning to organize its western acquisitions. California boundaries had been set, and the politically sensitive issue of slavery had been temporarily resolved in the Compromise of 1850 with the creation of New Mexico and Utah territories out of the previously undivided northern Mexico. Ultimately, Congress would carve Colorado, Utah, Nevada, Arizona, and New Mexico out of this region. But in the fall of 1851 the newly created territory of Utah stretched from California eastward to the crest of the Rocky Mountains and southward from the forty-second parallel to the present northern New Mexico boundary. It thus encompassed almost the entire range of both eastern and western Utes, which extended from northern New Mexico, through what would become western Colorado, and into most of Utah. What had once been a contiguous, unboundaried Mexican frontier had, since the Compromise of 1850, become two separate territories with two separate jurisdictions for administering Indian affairs.

Unaware of the significance of these political developments, Don Pedro León, the fifty-seven-year-old part-time farmer and Indian trader from Abiquiú, New Mexico, went to the new governor and superintendent of Indian affairs of New Mexico, James Calhoun, to secure a license to trade with the Yuta (Ute) Nation of Indians. The license was issued August 14, 1851, good until November, 14, 1851, on the posting of a thousand-dollar bond. Luján agreed that he and his "aids [*sic*], assistants, and servants" would comply with "all the rules and regulations, adopted or that may be adopted" by the United States for regulating the trade and intercourse with the Utah Indians. He was authorized to trade with the Ute Nation, "in their own localities," but only on his own private and individual account.[2]

The problem with this sweeping license was that the Utes' "own localities" were now almost totally inside Utah Territory. Technically, León's license was valid only

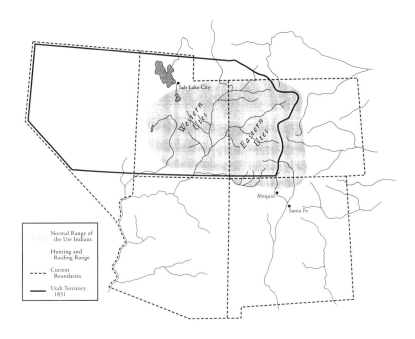

**2. UTAH TERRITORY AND THE RANGE OF UTE LANDS IN 1851**

in New Mexico, an impractical situation for a trader whose clients would be found almost exclusively outside that territory's boundary.

What is immediately obvious is Luján's lack of understanding of the United States' new territorial makeup and its significance for the legality of Indian trade. More surprising is Calhoun's appalling ignorance concerning at least one of the following: the extent of his jurisdiction, the legality of his issuing licenses to trade with Indians outside New Mexico, or the primary locations of the Ute Indians themselves. He was superintendent of Indian affairs in New Mexico—but it was Brigham Young who held authority over the Indians in Utah Territory (including the western slopes of the Rockies). The license issued to Luján by Calhoun authorized him to trade with the "Utah Nation of Indians . . . in their own localities." Although it could be argued that he might have assumed Luján intended to trade only with Utes in northern New Mexico or in the San Luis Valley, other actions argue differently. Calhoun had already issued at least one other license (July 1851) that specifically authorized its bearer to trade within "the Salt Lake country, in the Territory of Utah for the purpose of trading . . . with no other than Utah Indians." Eighteen months later another license would be issued by John Greiner, the new Indian superintendent, authorizing C. A. W. Bowman to trade "with the Utahs tribe of Indians . . . between Grand [Colorado] and Green Rivers," a region that lay completely within the boundaries of Utah Territory. As for whom the license authorized to trade, Luján may have understood the terms of the license to cover any member of his company under the sobriquet of "aids, assistants, and servants"—although this may be a stretch for even this illiterate, though not unintelligent, trader.[3]

### ATTEMPTS TO TRADE LEGALLY

Regardless, the trader and his company set out from New Mexico in September 1851, stopping to exchange their trade goods on "the other side" (east) of the Río Grande, possibly the San Luis Valley, where a number of other traders were likewise engaged. Here the Mexicans traded for horses, mules, and highly valued Ute-tanned buckskins.[4]

After trading for these goods, Luján headed a company of traders who turned westward to take their horses and mules to barter with the central Utah Utes.[5] There is no question that their intention was to trade for captive Indian children, since they constituted the major item of western Ute trade, and that horses and armaments were what the Mexicans offered in exchange.[6] After arriving at the Green River crossing, a half dozen of the traders left with Luján to locate the governor and ex officio superintendent of Indian affairs, Brigham Young, to display their license to trade and to determine "if it was good to trade with the whites and Indians also, and if the license was not good, to endeavor to get one from the Governor."[7]

Luján faced two problems. First, his license was due to expire in a few weeks, on November 14. He probably hoped simply to renew his license, but he may also have suspected that the governor of Utah might wish to issue his own trading license instead. What the traders don't seem to have grasped was the significance of the territorial boundaries and the problem of jealously protected political jurisdictions. Felipe Archuleta, one of the traders, testified that they had a license from an officer in New Mexico giving them "permission to trade with the Utah

*7. Mexican trader on the Old Spanish Trail, 1846. From George Douglas Brewerton,* Overland with Kit Carson: A Narrative of the Old Spanish Trail in '48.

Indians, [but] he did not know there was any line in the Territories to restrict him from going anywhere."[8] This is not surprising, since before September 1850—when their last trading expedition would have taken place—there had been no line.

Mormons would maintain, and historians continue to write, that Brigham Young's contingent stumbled on the traders in Sanpete Valley as they pursued their "nefarious traffic" and took the opportunity to "strictly prohibit . . . further traffic."[9] Such was not the case. According to the Mexicans' affidavits, Luján and his companions spent a good deal of time trying to seek out the Utah governor and Indian superintendent in order to follow legal form for their trade.

First Luján traveled toward Great Salt Lake City, but at the Provo River a man told him Brigham Young was absent on a tour of the southern settlements.

Concerned with the political and civil organization of the young territory, Young had just established the new settlement of Nephi, had chosen the location for the new territorial capital at Fillmore, and had proceeded to Manti, where his companion, the Honorable Zerubbabel Snow, judge of the First District Court of Utah, was to set up the Second Judicial Court.

After following Young's company as far as the Sevier River, Luján was told the governor had left for Sanpete Valley. So he rejoined his company, the twenty-one Mexican traders and their seven servants, along with packs of buckskins and nearly a hundred horses, where they waited for him in the same Sanpete Valley.[10] Perhaps the trader found meeting Young there to be a fortuitous circumstance, since that was near where the group had expected to trade anyway.[11]

On November 3 Luján approached Governor Young with his license and the request that he and his group be allowed to trade with both the whites and the Indians.[12] Unfortunately, the Mexicans spoke no English and the Mormons spoke no Spanish. The sole interpreter available appears to have been Daniel W. Jones, a well-known Indian interpreter but only a fair speaker of Spanish. In Young's words, "there not being a good Spanish Interpreter present it was difficult to find out the real design or extent of their mission." Despite the language difficulties, however, Young determined—and probably rightly so—that the goal of the Mexicans was to trade horses and mules for Indian children, a trade that had "been carried on for many years back." At this point the Utah governor and superintendent of Indian affairs "pointedly forbade" the Mexicans to trade with the Indians—for anything. He instructed them in the evils of the Indian slave trade and told them that their license was not valid in Utah Territory; to conduct any kind of trade with the Indians without a new and valid license—which he refused to issue—would mean that they would be violating the Trade and Intercourse Act regulating trade with the Indians within the United States. They were permitted to trade with the whites and to obtain provisions for their return trip. The Mexicans, all "employed by Mr. Pedro León, as Clerks, Servants, traders etc.," promised to return home. Luján would later complain that he was refused the license "on the grounds that he was not a Mormon."[13]

## TROUBLE WITH THE INDIANS

At this point, with his thousand-dollar bond at stake, León and his traders made preparations to return to New Mexico and abandoned their plans to trade with the

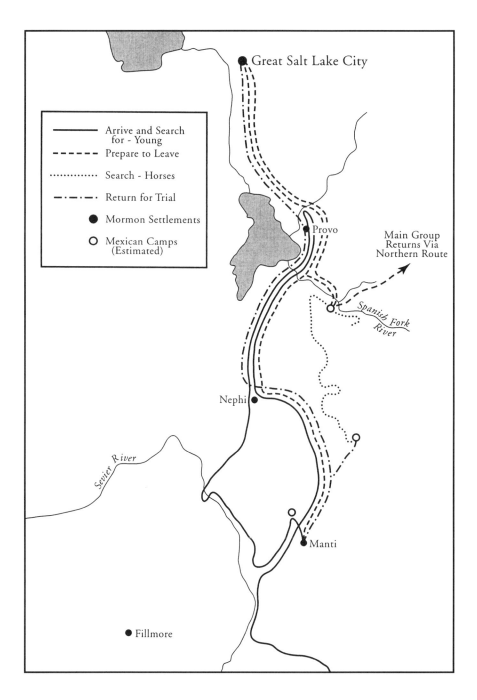

Legend:

Arrive and Search for - Young
Prepare to Leave
Search - Horses
Return for Trial
● Mormon Settlements
○ Mexican Camps (Estimated)

Great Salt Lake City

Provo

Main Group Returns Via Northern Route

Spanish Fork River

Nephi

Sevier River

Manti

● Fillmore

3. CENTRAL UTAH AND PROBABLE ROUTES OF PEDRO LEÓN LUJÁN AND HIS TRADING PARTY

Indians. But the Indians who were expecting to trade with the Mexicans had different ideas. While the Mexicans were still in Sanpete following Young's refusal to grant them a license, the company was approached by at least one party of Utes, with whom they refused to trade. Angry at the refusal, these Indians stole five or six horses. The traders complained to Stephen B. Rose, the Mormon Indian sub-agent for the area. He ordered George Bean, another Mormon Indian interpreter, to see if he could recover the horses and mules from the Indians to return to the Mexicans, but Bean was unsuccessful. Fearful of repeated thefts and greater inroads into whatever profits this trading trip would see, Luján moved the company north to the Spanish Fork River and decided to let this loss go.[14]

Leaving the majority of the party to watch the horses, Luján and a few companions went to Great Salt Lake City to purchase provisions. But on his return, about November 11 or 12, he discovered that Indians had stolen another six animals three days earlier. Unwilling to accept this additional loss, he instructed the majority of the party to pack up and leave immediately for Santa Fe by way of the northerly Spanish Fork route, taking with it most of the stock and provisions. Luján kept only enough horses, mules, and supplies to allow himself and seven others to locate their missing animals and catch up with the rest of the group. After retrieving their animals, they planned to overtake the main company by following the regular route through Sanpete Valley and along the traditional trader's trail through the mountains at Salina Canyon.[15]

The Mexicans testified that they sought for and received permission from "Mormon authorities" to search for the lost animals,[16] and for the next three weeks Luján and his companions did just that. Their first discovery yielded only the hides of two of the horses, the Indians having already eaten them. When the Indians were unable either to restore or to pay for the missing horses, Vicente Chaves, the owner, accepted a thirty-year-old captive Indian woman as compensation. Later Miguel Archuleta would also be forced to accept a child in payment for one of his horses, likewise devoured. On another occasion Arapeen rode abruptly into the New Mexicans' camp, caught up five horses belonging to Miguel Archuleta, and threw down two Indian children, stating that "if he [Archuleta] had a mood to trade he would trade and if he had not he would trade any how." Another warrior caught a horse belonging to Albino Mestes, threw down a child, and rode off without bothering to comment at all.[17]

The unlucky traders continued to follow the tracks of some of their stolen animals. They located a band of Indians and charged them with the theft, but although the Indians finally acknowledged they had the horses, they refused to return them and insisted the Mexicans take a boy and girl in their place. Despite demanding the return of their stock so that they could have pack animals and transportation to get home, the Mexicans were forced to take the children in lieu of the horses or forfeit payment entirely. Luján would later claim there had been nearly three hundred Indians in the band against his eight, though this is probably an exaggeration. He would also assert that his intentions were to take the captives back to New Mexico, where he would present his case to Governor Calhoun, ask for indemnity for his lost horses, and leave the disposal of the captives to the government[18]—although this seems rather too altruistic given his years-long profession.

Whatever his intentions, Luján's experiences were certainly not new. Mormons themselves had already been unwilling participants in coercive sales of Indian children from Ute slavers, and Mauricio Arze and Lagos García had been forced in 1813 to accept Indian captives instead of the furs they wanted.

### THE ARREST

Such precedents would not save the traders in Luján's company, however. On December 5 or 6, while the Spaniards were camped on Salt Creek about a half day's journey from Manti in Sanpete Valley, local Indians informed officials at Manti that the Mexican traders were still around and had Indian captives in their possession. A warrant for their arrest on the charge of trading with the Indians without a license was issued by a local justice of the peace. The Mexicans were arrested by a posse of some forty men led by George Peacock, who confiscated their horses, mules, tack, and Indian captives and took the traders into custody.

In Manti they were unsuccessfully represented before the justice of the peace by a sympathetic new attorney, Andrew Siler. From the beginning the Mexicans feared they would have a difficult time receiving a fair trial in Utah. Juan Antonio Baldineros complained to Siler that James T. S. Allred, the Manti prosecutor, was their enemy and that he was trying "to injure them by getting the Indians to Testify against them."[19] After the case was transferred to the First District Court in Great Salt Lake City, Siler continued as an interested party to the action, writing to the new attorneys that he felt "no interest further than this, I want to see justice between man & man and Pedro Leon & Co. want me to do all I can for them." He also told them that they should "tell them [the Mexicans] that I have employed you and they will have all the confidence imaginable in you. They think considerable of me and were much chagrined when I told them that I couldn't go to Salt Lake with them." He sent Francis Pomeroy as an interpreter whom both the new attorneys and the Mexicans could trust, "as he is an Amigo to them."[20]

Siler also offered background and personal advice on the case. He, too, was particularly concerned with the subpoenaing of Indian witnesses. Not only were the Indians, as parties to the transactions, equally guilty under the law, but they were also interested parties who stood to gain if the Mexicans were found guilty. They may have thought (or may have been led to believe) there was a possibility they could reclaim the forfeited children if the traders were found guilty. Arapeen was already claiming that he had traded a child for the Spanish horse he was riding around the community at the time of the Manti trial; Juan Antonio Baldineros denied the trade, however, contending that the horse in question had actually been stolen "out of the corell [*sic*] at this place after the Spaniards were in jail & their horses in the custody of the sheriff."[21]

On December 9 the local court sent word to Judge Snow in Great Salt Lake City that they had found the Spanish traders guilty of "the crime of trading with the Indians of this County & Territory without license."[22] Stephen B. Rose, the Indian sub-agent, was sent to investigate. On his return to Great Salt Lake City, he made an affidavit to the First District Court on which the clerk issued a warrant for the arrest of Luján and the members of his company.[23] Marshal Joseph L. Heywood was sent to bring the Mexicans (and their confiscated property, now "officially" seized by an officer of the court) to Great Salt Lake City to be tried before the First District Court.[24]

## THE TRIAL

At the time of the trial both New Mexico and Utah territories were in the midst of political change and controversy. Both had been created as part of a congressional compromise on the issue of whether the new Mexican acquisitions would enter the Union as slave or free. Utah, populated predominantly by northerners, was expected to enter as free. On the other hand, the question of slavery was a great

*8. Joseph L. Heywood. Courtesy of the Utah State Historical Society.*

deal more complicated in New Mexico. On the surface New Mexico appeared to be a prime candidate for the expansion of slavery; after all, it lay due west of traditional slave states and it already used tens of thousands of debt-bondage peons or Indian "slaves."

But half of New Mexico had become a political bone caught between two snarling dogs: Texas versus the population centers along the Río Grande in New Mexico.[25] Texas had bided its time through the Mexican War to press its boundary claims along the Río Grande all the way to its headwaters in Colorado—a move that would have taken half of New Mexico and placed Santa Fe in Texas. Knowing this, New Mexico made an immediate bid for statehood along with California in 1848 and thumbed its nose at its slave-state neighbor by passing a memorial opposing slavery. Texas, on the other hand, began vigorously to assert its claims to the territory east of the Río Grande by legislating a county organization and judicial district, asserting control over the Santa Fe militia, providing for "Santa Fe district" representation in the Texas House of Representatives, and sending a judge to Santa Fe. New Mexico responded by ignoring the Texas judge as much as possible and then, in early 1850, calling for a constitutional convention and drafting a constitution that, among other things, would have officially banned slavery.

Texas was enraged, threatening both an invasion of New Mexico and secession from the Union when a vacillating federal government finally sanctioned New Mexico's petition and then threatened military reprisals against Texas if New Mexico were attacked. The Texas–New Mexico controversy became almost as volatile an issue to be resolved in the Compromise of 1850 as the issue of slavery. The explosive question of Texas's boundary and the issue of slave-state balance was finally resolved with the 1850 congressional compromise: Texas was compensated for the loss of New Mexican territory, and New Mexico and Utah were established as new territories with popular sovereignty left to each of them in deciding the issue of slavery.

With the boundary dispute resolved and the territory's labor needs already being met with their slave-like peons, however, New Mexicans suddenly seemed to grow apathetic toward the question of slavery. They had, after all, been more anti-Texas than anti-slave. By 1857 there was no need to vote either territory slave or free, for the Dred Scott decision had spread de facto slavery throughout the United States. By 1859 an increasingly pro-South New Mexican legislature—one that also may have hoped to validate its own rampant system of debt bondage—would respond to this decision by passing slave codes to regulate the treatment and punishment of black slaves and codify (and accept, unlike the North at this time) the already existing regulations under the Fugitive Slave Act providing for the return of runaway black slaves (although the 1860 census still listed no slaves in New Mexico).[26]

But in 1851–52, when Pedro León Luján came to trial in Utah, New Mexico was still on the record opposing slavery, while the question of slavery remained a politically sensitive issue in Utah Territory yet to be resolved.

Utah Territory also faced another ongoing conflict, that of the feud between Mormon and non-Mormon officials. Shortly after the creation of the territory the

*9. Great Salt Lake City, 1853. Courtesy of the Utah State Historical Society.*

control of the Utah civil judiciary was shifted to a supreme court made up of the federally appointed justices who were to preside over the territory's three judicial districts. These civil courts were to adjudicate non-Mormon cases or criminal actions (Mormons were expected to have their misunderstandings arbitrated by ecclesiastical courts). When many of the federally appointed gentile officials arrived in Utah, however, they found themselves almost immediately embroiled in conflicts with the Mormon leaders.[27] In mid-September 1851—about the time Luján's traders were arriving—many of these non-Mormon officials fled the territory to take their complaints to Washington (Utah's "runaway officials"). Among those who had just left were Judges Perry E. Brocchus and Lemuel G. Brandebury, leaving Zerubbabel Snow, a Mormon, the only remaining district judge in Utah. Shortly thereafter the legislature extended broad probate jurisdiction, and Judge Snow was authorized to serve in all three districts until new judges could be appointed by the president. This move, however, left the territory without a supreme court to which district cases could have been appealed. It also left the state with a civil court system still heavily dominated by Mormons.[28] Indeed, all the major Utah officials who were involved with the Mexicans' case were Mormon.

## COURT OFFICIALS

Judge Zerubbabel Snow presided. Snow, one of the first associate justices on the federal courts in Utah, would later be elected by the legislature as attorney general. After he was forced into retirement in 1874, he remained prominent, often defending Mormons on polygamy charges, including Brigham Young.[29]

The United States was represented by the prosecuting U.S. attorney for the Territory of Utah, Seth M. Blair. The first U.S. attorney appointed for the new Utah Territory, Blair was a southerner and a long-standing foe of Mexicans. He had been a major in the Texas Rangers, fighting in the Texas war of independence against Mexico, and was a veteran of the Mexican-American War. Daniel Jones remembered the prosecutor as wise, tactful, and "knowing all about the Mexican character, having been in the Texan war." He was also a man of decided prejudices against blacks and Mexicans.[30]

The defense attorneys for the Mexican traders were George A. Smith (counsel) and Josiah Slayton and William Pickett (assistant defense counselors). Smith, like Siler, had been practicing law only since early October 1851. He had also only recently returned from helping found settlements in southern Utah, where he and his neighbors were all actively purchasing Indian children. He was acquainted with the notorious slaver, Wákara, from whom members of the settlements frequently bought children. His own first encounter with the southern Utah Indians had occurred early in the year when Indians had slaughtered one of his oxen and Smith had asked them to give him a twelve-year-old Paiute boy in compensation. By 1853 (a year after the trial) one non-Mormon traveler noted that almost every Mormon family in southern Utah had one or two Indian children they had purchased from the Indians.[31]

The court also called a jury of "good and lawful men" from Great Salt Lake City. William McBride, a forty-five-year-old blacksmith, acted as foreman. Others were common laborers, a shoemaker, a stonecutter, and a doctor.[32] George Bean acted as interpreter for the Indian witnesses, and Francis Pomeroy served as Spanish interpreter.[33]

## COURT PROCEEDINGS

The trial of the Mexican traders had been set for January 5, 1852, but on their arrival in Great Salt Lake City, they promptly petitioned the court for a speedy trial. As a

*10. Zerubbabel Snow. Courtesy of the Utah State Historical Society.*

result, Judge Snow moved the trial date up a week and ordered a special session of court to be held beginning on Monday, December 29.[34] At that time the officers of the court, the defendants, and their counselor, Smith, appeared before the court and preliminary motions were filed and subpoenas issued for the first of a series of witnesses. Among those subpoenaed by Blair as witnesses for the state were the

*11. Seth M. Blair. Courtesy of the Utah State Historical Society.*

original arresting officer, George Peacock, and the Manti prosecutor, James T. S. Allred (although neither appeared), as well as the Indian traders Arapeen and Sequite and both Indian and Spanish interpreters, George Bean and Francis Pomeroy.

Blair then filed formal motions against the traders, first a libel action "in a declaration of Debt against the Property of the said Pedro Leon & others" confiscated as part of the ongoing legal action. This case of libel required a

*12. George A. Smith. Courtesy of the Utah State Historical Society.*

fourteen-day notification before it could be tried in the court—which it was on January 15–17, 1852—and was published in the *Deseret News Weekly* and posted on the courthouse door. Blair followed this motion by filing a "Petition in Debt" for the five-hundred-dollar fine required for violating the Trade and Intercourse Act regulating trade with the Indians and for which all the traders' merchandise (including their horses and mules) had become forfeit.

The next day, December 30, the jury was impaneled and sworn in without challenge. Smith filed a "Plea of Denial of Debt" on behalf of Luján and the others, and the trial began. The first witness for the prosecution was the veteran Indian slave trader Arapeen, who testified with George Bean as his interpreter. His testimony stretched through the morning and well into the afternoon, after which the court heard additional evidence presented by Albert Carrington, the interpreters Francis Pomeroy and George Bean, and finally Governor Brigham Young.

That afternoon and into December 31 the defense examined its own witnesses, Felipe Santiago Archuleta and Antonio Jose Griego, through two interpreters, Daniel Jones and Francis Pomeroy. The trial ended with a final testimony offered, for the prosecution, by Daniel Jones.

The trial came to a close that afternoon as both attorneys made their concluding arguments to the court and jury. Slayton, assistant counsel for the defense, tried to object to the use of Arapeen's testimony but was overruled; then he addressed the court and made his plea for the traders. The trial concluded as Blair stood to make the prosecution's final arguments before the court and jury. The jury was duly instructed by the court and, under the direction of bailiff Isaac Morley (a leader in the San Pete settlements), retired at five o'clock in the afternoon to deliberate. The next morning, January 1, 1852, William McBride, foreman, delivered the verdict of the jury, that it had found "the Defendant Don Pedro indebted to the United States."

### INTENT OF THE TRIAL

The trial had been held to determine whether or not the New Mexican traders had traded with the Utah Indians without a license, thus violating the Trade and Intercourse Act of 1834. This act had been originally passed by the U.S. Congress to regulate commercial intercourse in the newly created Indian country west of the Mississippi. If found guilty, the Mexicans would be fined five hundred dollars and their merchandise confiscated. At the time of the trial the court had in its possession, and the United States claimed forfeiture of, ten mules, six horses, a "squaw" (thirty years old) and eight Indian children (seven to twelve years old), and some miscellaneous "goods, wares, [and] merchandise."[35]

After hearing the testimony and the arguments of the attorneys, members of the jury were instructed by the court that if they determined from the evidence that the defendants had, without a license, introduced horses and mules into the "usual hunting ranges" of the Indians with the intent to trade with the Indians, their verdict should be guilty and the claims of the United States upheld. But if they found that the Spaniards had come into the territory with the intent of obtaining a license and then, and not until then, of trading with the Indians, they should be found not guilty. And if they also found that the "alleged" trading had been forced on the Spaniards by the Indians, this kind of trading would not fall within the definitions of trade regulated by the Trade and Intercourse Act of 1834, and they could not be found guilty of violating it. But if in the opinion of the jury the claims of the traders were simply a "device to evade the law," the trade would fall within the act and the Spaniards should be found guilty of trading without a license.[36]

## ARGUMENTS

A number of arguments were made in the defense of the Mexicans, specifically the question of the legality of Luján's license and how willful the trade had been. Peripheral to the case were other arguments to determine the legality of the prosecution itself. These included defining the legality of slavery per se, and Indian slavery in particular, and defining Indian country and the legality of trading in it.

### LEGALITY OF THE LICENSE

The first point to be determined by the court was the legality of Luján's license and the validity of the rest of the company to trade under that license, if it had been valid.

The court found that only Luján had ever had any kind of a valid license, and that one was good only for himself since it stated it was issued on "his own private and individual account." The other traders apparently were not "his aids, assistants, and servants" despite the court having called them "his clerks, servants, and traders." In any case, Luján's license was invalid for trade outside New Mexico since James Calhoun had no authority to issue a license for trade in Utah Territory. As for one trader who carried a *blank* license, the court found that it could be valid only if "blank be somebody, and somebody be blank."

### WILLFULNESS OF THE TRADE

The next point to be determined was whether or not the traders had willfully traded with the Indians without a valid license. The Mexicans argued that they had entered the country with the intent either to use or to extend Luján's existing license, or to obtain a new license if necessary, before trading with the Indians. Luján had, after all, chased the governor from Salt Lake to the Sevier River and back to Sanpete before trading. After the license was denied, the Mexicans claimed they had thereafter refused to trade with the Indians, which had resulted in the theft of six of their animals and the disappearance of another five or six later. This, in turn, had forced Luján and the other defendants to remain behind in an attempt to recover their losses. The traders also argued that they had intended to return to New Mexico after they were refused a license to trade, and indeed the majority of the party had left to return there within two weeks. The Indian captives in their possession, they insisted, had been forced on them against their will and were taken only when no other means of compensation for lost stock was available to them.

The prosecutor's argument lay primarily on the prima facie evidence of the confiscated Indian captives—proof that the Mexicans must have traded with the Indians—and on the testimony given by the Indian trader, Arapeen. Slayton did attempt to have Arapeen's testimony impeached, for, as the defense attorneys had been advised by Siler, the wily Ute was not the most trustworthy witness and may have been tampered with before the trial. The court overruled his objections, however, and the Indian trader's testimony stood. Consequently, the defense counsel was forced to fall back upon arguments over technicalities of the law.

Although the court minutes do not record the precise arguments used by the prosecutor, it is obvious from the published court findings that they attacked the defense of the Mexicans that they had been forced to make the exchange for captives. The only way the traders could be found guilty of violating the 1834 Indian trade laws was if the jury determined that they had willfully traded after having been refused licenses to trade in Utah, and that their story of being forced to accept the captives was only a means of circumventing the law. Since the Mexicans did not have a valid license but did have Indian slaves in their possession, the question boiled down to whether or not the jury believed their story of forced trade.

Apparently, the jury did not. Its verdict was swift and unequivocal that the defendant, "Don Pedro Leon" was guilty of "trading illegally with the Indians" and therefore indebted to the United States.[37] The horses, mules, tack, buckskins, and Indian captives were remanded to Marshal Heywood's care until after the cases of libel and indebtedness were determined two weeks later. At that time the defense attorneys filed motions to recover some of their clients' confiscated property under various irregularities of procedure and technicalities of the law, as well as filing at least two motions for retrial on the basis of new information or irregularities in the first proceedings. Meanwhile, the defense attorneys also filed a petition of habeas corpus on behalf of the Indian captives seeking their freedom.

## THE QUESTION OF SLAVERY

Shortly after the verdict was rendered, William Pickett, acting as attorney for the Indian captives now, petitioned the court under a writ of habeas corpus to free the Indian captives confiscated as property of the Mexican traders. Although a law passed earlier in 1851 had already established the proprietary and ownership rights of black slaves, the legal status of Indian slaves was yet to be determined.[38] The Mexicans had long since waived their ownership rights, but the prosecuting attorney was asking that the Indians be sold, along with the tack, buckskins, mules, and horses, to pay court costs, as black slaves could have been.

Blair argued that slavery was legal in the United States, depending on individual state laws. According to the Treaty of Guadalupe Hidalgo, all the laws of Mexico in force at the time of the Mexican cession continued in force therein *unless specifically changed*; Blair (erroneously) argued that since the Indian slave trade was a long-standing practice of the Mexicans and had not been made illegal in Utah, Indian slavery, like black slavery, must be legal. Therefore, the slaves confiscated with the rest of the Mexicans' merchandise were property that could be disposed of for value by the court.

Ironically, Blair's arguments were specious: not only had specific laws against Indian slavery been issued for Spanish American possessions in the early sixteenth century, but the buying and selling of Indian captives had been illegal in Spanish/Mexican territories—and thus also in the newly created New Mexico and Utah territories—since 1812. Indeed, the very traveling into Ute country by Spaniards for trade or barter had been made illegal in 1778.[39] Even James Calhoun, who signed Luján's license, had been attempting to control the slave trade through New Mexican laws, calling the trade "exceedingly pernicious" and "the greatest curse" on the Indians of the territory, recommending that the Trade and Intercourse Act be applied there, and issuing his own regulations in the meantime forbidding the trade.

Although the Spanish/Mexican laws had been continuously and regularly flouted and judicially ignored, technically the laws of Mexico that had extended over Utah after the Treaty of Guadalupe Hidalgo—not to mention the new New Mexican regulations—made the trading for slaves not legal, as Blair argued, but illegal![40]

In any case, Judge Snow based his decision strictly on American law. The judge could find no U.S. laws or acts of Congress recognizing Indian slavery, although Congress did allow a territory to *introduce* slavery. But Judge Snow reasoned that the right to introduce slavery was far different from exercising that right. Utah had never passed an act allowing Indian slavery and did not recognize Indian "tradition" as binding on its territorial laws, and thus the Indian captives seized from Luján's company were ordered released.

Since the children could hardly be returned to their unknown parents, however, they were placed in Mormon homes to be raised, as was customary whenever Indian children had been obtained through various means. Two of these children may have been Ellen Thomas, an Indian girl placed in the home of Elijah Thomas, a business associate of both Marshal Heywood and Seth Blair, and Kate Kimball, who was placed with Thomas's neighbors; both girls would have been about eight years old in 1852.[41] An irate León would claim that after confiscating them from him, these Indian children had been "sold to the Mormons as servants, by the Mormon Authorities."[42]

With this decision a precedent had been set. Within a month the Utah territorial legislature would pass an act making Indian slavery specifically illegal but setting out the procedure for purchasing Indian children as indentured servants, the indenture to last not longer than twenty years.[43] Ironically, it was a longer indenture than tradition prescribed for most Indians purchased in New Mexico.

## THE QUESTION OF INDIAN COUNTRY

One of the major arguments Smith and Slayton tried to make addressed the very question of the definition of Indian country. Indian country had to be defined since the Trade and Intercourse Act under which the Mexicans were accused applied to and regulated trade only in Indian country; in order to have violated the act the Mexicans must, therefore, be proved to have traded in Indian country.

Since 1763 and Britain's attempt to limit colonial expansion and to reduce friction with the Indians west of the Appalacians, Indian counry had been considered any area west of colonized regions. Attempts to regulate the "trade and intercourse" in Indian country had been made as early as 1790, and temporary measures continued to be passed from time to time. By 1830 Indian country—or Indian Territory—had become a place to which eastern Indians could be removed and concentrated. It had been reduced and defined as that area west of Arkansas and Missouri and south of the one hundredth parallel and the Missouri River. The western and southern boundaries were the general limits of the United States: the one hundredth meridian and the Texas border. With the expansion of the country's western borders in 1848 following the Mexican War, the country also acquired new, unsettled Indian country. Although the Trade and Intercourse Act of 1834 had intended only to regulate the trade within the ever-changing boundaries of Indian Territory, after 1848 the laws were extended over the new western territories as part of the government's ongoing attempts to monitor and regulate Indian-white relations.

The court in Utah faced some interesting dilemmas in its attempt to define Indian country. If Indian country was to be defined as territory reserved exclusively for the occupancy of Indians (which the establishment of Indian country in 1830 seemed to intend), then all the settlements in Utah would necessarily be illegal if the territory were Indian country. The attorneys for the defense argued that the initial settlements had been made before Utah was part of the United States or during the Mexican War; when Congress made Utah a territory, however, it had validated the legality of the settlements there. Since Indian country must be administered under the jurisdiction of Congress, it must, then, be an area separate from any state or territorial jurisdiction. If Indian country regulations were to extend over all the settlements, then all trade, even by the settlers, must be considered illegal. Indeed, since Utah Territory existed in the midst of Indian lands, unoccupied by anyone save Indians, simply to travel to Utah through the Indian territories would be to "introduce" illegal merchandise into Indian country.

Simply put, if Utah Territory were deemed Indian country and trading therefore illegal, then all white settlements, trading, and travel through it was illegal (including that done by the Mormons). Since the court could hardly make that finding (no territorial court could have), then Utah Territory must not be Indian country and thus not liable to the regulations of the Trade and Intercourse Act of 1834. If, therefore, Utah were not Indian country, then how could the Mexicans be tried for violating the Trade and Intercourse Act at all?

On the other hand, Blair argued for the prosecution that according to the treaty of Guadalupe Hidalgo, California, New Mexico, and Utah were subject to the same Indian rights of occupancy with the same regulations that prevailed in the rest of the United States. Because the Indians' rights of occupancy had never been extinguished, and because the territory was wholly occupied by Indians, the entire territory should be considered Indian country.

Thus, one of the major questions addressed in this case was the definition of Indian country in a region in which white settlements were vying for occupancy with the Indians and in which an ongoing trade between white settlers and neighboring Indians was quite naturally occurring. This was important, of course, in determining the guilt of the Mexican traders, yet that seems to have become almost of peripheral significance in the findings of the court. What was at stake was much more than a five-hundred-dollar fine against a few Mexican traders; the legality of the Mormons' settlements and their trade and missionary work among the Indians in an "Indian country" could be called into question.

In attempting to define the legal position of Utah Territory in being or not being Indian country under the definition of the Trade and Intercourse Act of 1834, Judge Snow was forced to argue his way through a morass of theoretical definitions of what Indian country was when it was not specifically the bounded Indian country that had been created in 1830.

Ultimately, Judge Snow neatly sidestepped the entire issue of Indian country and the question of "sole occupancy." An Act of Congress, February 27, 1851, had extended all U.S. laws then in force regulating trade and intercourse with the Indian *tribes* (not *country*) over Utah and New Mexico. The word *tribe* was understood to mean the people themselves, whereas the word *country* was understood to mean the land they occupied to the exclusion of whites. Obviously, Utah, and other new territories, could not fall within the intended meaning of Indian country, because although Indians occupied the country and their rights of occupancy had not been extinguished, they did not occupy it to the exclusion of whites. To extend the Trade and Intercourse Act over such territories could not have been the intent of the Congress. If it had, then all white settlements in, and even the travel of emigrants through, Indian lands would be illegal because they would have "introduced into the regular hunting grounds" of the Indians potential merchandise that could be traded or sold. Perhaps even trade between whites themselves could be deemed illegal.

Turning to the Constitution, Judge Snow found that the federal government was authorized to "regulate commerce with foreign nations, . . . among states . . . and with Indian Tribes." Thus, Judge Snow reasoned, the *intent* of the federal laws—and the Trade and Intercourse Act of 1834—was to regulate the trade between whites and Indians, whether in a regularly bounded "country" or not. The Trade and Intercourse Act of 1834 was extended, through constitutional *intention*, to mean the regulation of trade between whites and Indians in any territory or state in the Union. Therefore, Luján and the other Mexican traders could be held liable for trading with Indians without a license while in Utah, and more important, Mormon settlements could legally continue to expand throughout Utah's Indian lands. As for Mormon transactions with the Indians, the implication was that they, being sanctioned by the Utah government (and apparently without the need of a formal license), were legal.

Despite these circumlocutions and excursions through the technicalities of law and language, Judge Snow never successfully defined the relationship that must continue between Mormon whites and the Indians in whose lands they were expanding. The Mexican traders would be found guilty of trading with the Indians without a license, having deliberately introduced trade goods into the Indians' "regular hunting grounds and camps" for that purpose. And yet the Utah Mormons would continue to have commercial "trade and intercourse" with the Indians for years to come, not only for food, stock, or clothing but for Indian children as well—all without licenses and without fear of arrest or seizure of goods. Mexicans, on the other hand, if caught doing the same thing, faced arrest, confiscation of property, and summary expulsion.[44] This very point would later be exploited by non-Mormon Indian agents, who would point to Mormon trade and missionary work among the Indians as being carried on without a license within "Indian country" and use it as a means of attacking the Mormons in hopes of severing their relations with the Indians.[45]

### APPEALS AND PETITIONS

Luján continued his appeals for a new trial and a reexamination of evidence, his actions those of a man who believed in his innocence and felt he had been wronged. Even after returning to New Mexico he would continue to solicit testimony from resident whites as to the non-slave status of Indian children sold in

New Mexico and southern Colorado, and petition redress from New Mexican and Washington officials.[46]

The first petition made by Luján's defense counsel was to have the verdict reversed and a new trial set based on irregularities in the arrest and seizure procedures and on the question of the court's jurisdiction. The property of the traders had originally been seized by men having no jurisdiction to do so, and the Mexicans had been arrested within the jurisdiction of the Second Judicial Court (newly created the month before by Judge Snow himself), not the First.[47]

The court found the technicalities raised by Smith and Slayton to be irrelevant. Stephen B. Rose, as an Indian agent, was an agent of the government and could act independently within his jurisdiction. Like revenue agents who could arrest and seize goods on probable cause of illegal trading, an Indian agent, on his own authority, could arrest and seize the property of whites illegally trading with Indians under his jurisdiction. Once Rose made his affidavit to the court, December 13, the arrest and seizure could be viewed as having been made on his authority and the actions of Marshal Joseph Heywood as extensions of Rose's own actions. Though perhaps slightly irregular, Judge Snow argued, this was nevertheless within the acceptable limits of the law.

Again, because the case rightfully fell under the jurisdiction of the Indian agent, his authority allowed him to take his prisoners and goods to any legally recognized court within the state or territory of arrest. Thus, Rose had given the First District Court jurisdiction by virtue of his having made his complaint there.[48]

IRREGULARITY OF CONFISCATING HORSES AND PACK MULES

Undaunted, Smith and Slayton filed more petitions and initiated a countersuit against the state for illegally confiscating the Mexicans' horses and pack mules on the basis that property liable to seizure by the Act of 1834 did not include them within their definition of "merchandise"—a reasonable argument inasmuch as they were the traders' pack and riding animals. The court found, however, that since horses and mules were the merchandise brought to trade (and for which the Indians had traded), they fell within the definitions of "merchandise" in the act and were liable to forfeiture (despite these particular animals being the Mexicans' only means of transportation home).[49]

PREJUDICIAL JURY

Luján also filed a petition for retrial, claiming a prejudicial jury.[50] Daniel Jones noted in his memoirs that "a great deal of prejudice and bitter feeling was manifested toward the Mexicans." In mid-November the *Deseret News Weekly* printed an editorial in which it called Luján a liar, a traitor, and a kidnapper. He was a liar for claiming to have a license signed by Governor Calhoun. He was guilty of treason for selling or trading weapons to warring Navajos—or at least selling weapons destined for the Navajos (through the Ute trading connection)—and deserved "a traitor's halter." He was a kidnapper for attempting to carry Indian children out of the territory and should be tried for that crime, too.[51] If the *Deseret News Weekly* had had its way, Luján and company would have been jailed, fined, and hanged!

The prosecuting attorney also seems to have been personally prejudiced against the Mexicans. But what seems most damning was that at least one of the jurors had already declared the defendants guilty nearly a week before the trial began. James Ferguson, another attorney in Great Salt Lake City, filed a deposition stating that about a week before the trial, he had heard George D. Grant, a juror, at the home of Seth M. Blair, the prosecutor, declare that Luján and others of the "Spanish" company were guilty and ought to be punished. The possession of the Indian children was "sufficient evidence" of their having traded with the Indians.[52] The court apparently took no serious consideration of this new evidence.

CLAIM OF A NEW LICENSE TO TRADE

On January 9 Slayton filed one of the most interesting petitions in the record. He asked for a retrial on the basis of having just learned of material evidence unknown to the defense during the first trial. We can only speculate as to why the evidence was not introduced at first, perhaps because of the language barrier or simply an inadequate defense. Nevertheless, Slayton reported that around December 1—a month after Young had denied Luján a license to trade and nearly two weeks after Luján had sent his main company back to Santa Fe—Luján "did . . . Procure a

License of Stephen B. Rose an Indian Agent for said Territory authorizing and Permitting said León to Trade and Traffic with the Indian Tribes."[53] Since Rose was the complainant and "arresting" officer, it is difficult to imagine how or why he would have thought to issue a license to trade to a man whom he knew had been refused such a license by his superior. Did Luján actually have such a license? Some type of document must have existed, for Slayton was willing to offer it as evidence.

It is possible the Mexicans had been given some type of document allowing them to pursue the Indians who had stolen their stock and recover it or a reasonable compensation in lieu of it. Records do indicate early assistance from Mormon authorities. If so, the attorneys may have tried to parlay such a document into official permission to trade for unrecoverable stolen stock (which was what the Mexicans claimed they had done): perhaps an ad hoc trading license? The court took no action on the petition, however, and the mysterious document, having never been made a part of the record, has been lost.

Nevertheless, the implication that such a document existed raises a number of intriguing questions. Why would Luján ask for a license when he was ostensibly preparing to go home? Why would Rose even consider giving him such a license when the superintendent had refused to issue one only a month earlier? Could there have been collusion between Luján and Rose, which Rose would deny when he was called on to investigate the charge that Luján was trading without a license? If Rose had admitted issuing one, under the circumstances, it could have proved most embarrassing. Or was Don Pedro León lying? If so, who prepared the document for him, since he was illiterate? And if he was planning to go home without trading, why would he have tried to obtain a license behind Young's back? Would Slayton have filed a petition if he had not personally seen the purported license? The answers to these questions may never be known. The court ignored the petition, and Luján was not granted a retrial.

## TREATMENT OF THE MEXICANS
## AND THE ADEQUACY OF THEIR DEFENSE

Was the defense of the Mexicans adequate? The attorneys were, after all, court-appointed Mormon advocates. Yet these attorneys filed petition after petition on behalf of the traders based on technicalities of the law—though the court consistently brushed them aside—and even attempted (unsuccessfully) to countersue the state on behalf of their clients in order to recover their confiscated property. But since the key to their defense lay in their having been coerced into accepting the captives, did the attorneys sufficiently argue this aspect, using the many precedents of recent Mormon experience to prove that this was a common practice among the Utes? The court minutes do not answer this question, and the findings of the court all seem to be based on legal technicalities, scarcely touching on the coercive-sales aspect of the case. And, not the least, how significant was the language barrier to an effective defense of the Spanish-speaking Mexicans?

Luján's final attempt in the Mormon-dominated courts would be an attempt to sue the Mormons for his lost property and false imprisonment, but Brigham Young simply referred him to Washington. At last, after having exhausted all legal resorts, the Mexicans paid their fine. The court records indicate Luján was fined five hundred dollars (the mandatory fine by the Act of 1834); it is not clear if each trader was also fined that amount. Luján later reported to John Greiner, acting superintendent of Indian affairs in New Mexico, that each trader was fined only fifty dollars—an error in transcription?—"which was at once remitted." Since the fine was paid through the confiscation of the horses, mules, and tack, the traders had little choice in its remittance, of course. Court records refer to their having refused to pay their fines, but that may have been merely a legal formula for prosecuting the case of forfeiture.

Brigham Young, who was described as "treating the whole party with the greatest kindness, while they were in the Country," and as having tried to use his influence to provide a "fair and impartial trial," supplied provisions sufficient for the Mexicans' return home. The provisions did not, however, include transportation, so Luján and his companions were forced to return to Santa Fe on foot, through the mountains, in midwinter. They left February 6 and arrived in Abiquiú April 4, having "suffered a great deal from being caught in the snows in the Mountains—sometimes being compelled to wade in the snow to their armpits."[54] Within several weeks Luján had sought out depositions and made complaints to New Mexican authorities. But although letters were even sent to the commissioner of Indian Affairs, the disgruntled traders were to find little satisfaction there either.

Mexican traders, returning to Utah on their annual, and previously unmolested, trading expedition, found in 1851 a population no longer prepared to suffer their presence or their enterprise. When they were discovered with "merchandise" in their possession, whether innocently or surreptitiously obtained, the Mormon response was quick and decisive. The traders' only defense was that they had been coerced into accepting the Indian captives, but neither the public nor the court was prepared to be receptive to any of the arguments the Mexicans made in their defense. Despite the plethora of identical instances of coercive—and voluntary— purchases of Indian children by the Mormons over the previous four years, the Mormon court refused to believe that the Mexicans had been similarly compelled. There is no doubt that the purpose of the trip to Utah had been to trade for Indian captives—both Brigham Young's testimony and tradition validate that conclusion. Nevertheless, the Utah jurors could not be persuaded that, once having been denied permission to trade, these (or perhaps any) Mexicans would honor their word and pack up and leave the area without attempting to smuggle out a few captives. Despite their affidavits and personal testimony, and the evidence of their actions in sending most of the traders and goods home while preparing to leave themselves, the jury concluded that the Mexicans were lying to cover their having been caught "with the goods."

Adding insult to injury was the disposition of the captives, the possession of whom had brought the Mexicans to trial. The Mexicans had accepted their confiscation and had relinquished their claim to ownership for the trial. But then the Indians had been "freed" only to be sold into indentureship in Mormon homes; from Luján's perspective, the "Mormon authorities" had done precisely what he had been tried and convicted of attempting to do—taking Indian children to be sold into informal indentures and raised in homes as acculturated menials.[55]

From the point of view of the Mormon authorities, who had declared the Indian captives free and not property, they were simply placing the children into foster homes—under the new indenture law—since there was no practical way at that point of locating families and returning the captives to their parents. That is assuming that those parents were alive in any case and that the authorities saw past the opportunity of raising a few more acculturated Lamanites.

There is some justice in Luján's complaint that Brigham Young denied him a license to trade because he was not a Mormon.[56] León and company were tried for trading with the Indians for Indian children, a practice in which the Mormon populace was actively engaged and which their governor and church president had only recently advised them to do "as quickly as possible." The defending attorney, George A. Smith, had himself taken an Indian child only a few months before in recompense for an ox that had been stolen and butchered by an Indian, as the Mexicans' horses had been. Yet the court found the Mormon commerce in Indian children to be legal whereas the Mexican trade was not. The only difference Luján could perceive was racial and religious—he was a Catholic Mexican, not a Mormon Utahn. He was probably right.

What Luján could not have seen or understood, particularly given the New Mexican history of ignoring the problems caused by the slave trade, was that the political difficulties stemming from Indian slavery had to be stopped. That could be done only by banning Mexican trade expeditions through Utah exactly like his. Although the purchase of Indian captives might appear to be identical in practice, Mormon or Mexican, the difference really lay in the pernicious effects of the traditional Mexican trade in maintaining the hostilities between tribes. The Mexicans who used Indian menials in large numbers were willing to put up with occasional Indian raids as the price for having wild Indian tribes available as a source of servants. The Utahns did not have the luxury of accepting Indian hostilities, nor did they wish to. Their communities had been quickly spread out and were vulnerable. Though they accepted the voluntary placement of Indian children as much as possible for the purpose of acculturation, they realized a peaceful setting was necessary for both their Indian missionary and settlement efforts.

Don Pedro León, and all other Mexican traders of his ilk, endangered that peaceful settlement process. They stirred up hostility and provided arms, ammunition, and horses that helped perpetuate it. And most important, they created the market that kept alive the slave trade and its cruel Indian slave raids. The Mormons saw themselves not as creating a market for slaves but as absorbing and emancipating the captives already taken, or supplying homes for Indian children whose families were too destitute to provide for them.

Still, the bottom line of the court proceeding was the legality of trading with Indians, particularly for their captive children. Despite the inherent hypocrisy of convicting the Mexican traders of a "crime" in which the Mormon population itself was blatantly and actively participating (including court officials), the court action gave Utah officials the precedent on which they could base future regulatory and judicial action aimed at stopping the trade. Outsider, New Mexican trade with

Indians was forbidden, although local, Utah trade was allowed; Indians could not be enslaved, but Indian children could be purchased into a sometimes slavelike indenture from which they could be emancipated on their majority.

By managing the meaning of the carefully chosen terms to be used, the Utahns were able to manipulate the political necessities of Indian trade and slavery into an acceptable form of bonded servitude, at the same time precluding the outside trade they felt endangered their Mormon enclaves. Though successful in achieving these ends, the trial and subsequent curtailment of the Mexican trade on the Old Spanish Trail would also bring some unforeseen consequences to both Utah and New Mexico.

## CHAPTER SIX

## AFTERMATH OF THE TRIAL

The trial and subsequent curtailment of the Mexican trade on the Old Spanish Trail affected not only the traders themselves but also the political and military situations in both Utah and New Mexico. Utah institutionalized the purchase and indenturing of Indian children, open Mexican trade was effectively eliminated, and short-term Indian hostilities escalated, leading, in part, to a brief but bloody Indian war with the chief Indian traders. In New Mexico, where the demand for Indian servants had not diminished, traders turned increasingly to making their own slave raids, plundering Navajos to make up the difference in lost Paiute captives and increasing the level of hostilities on that Indian front.

### EFFECT ON PEDRO LEÓN LUJÁN

On a personal level the trial and its verdict were financially disastrous for the leader of the trading expedition, Pedro León Luján. Though we do not have specific figures to reflect Luján's losses, their relative severity can be estimated based on his subsequent actions. Luján had a substantial amount of money invested in the trading venture to begin with, including the trade goods necessary to initiate the expedition as well as the one-thousand-dollar bond he had to post to get his trading license.

The caravan that headed to Utah with Luján included disparate traders who either had joined up under Luján's guide or direction or had banded together for mutual protection. We may assume that the trade goods held by each one were his own, and any profits accrued remained his. How much of the pack train that returned early to New Mexico belonged to Luján can only be guessed at. If Luján and the other defendants who remained in Utah kept their own goods with them, as they may have done (they still had the buckskins with them from their southern Ute trade), then they would have lost everything they had invested in that year's expedition; all pack animals, equipment, and buckskins that were not initially stolen by the Indians were confiscated by the court to pay their fines. The

Mexicans had to return home on foot, their only supplies provided through the charity of Brigham Young.

Since the traders were convicted in a court of law of having violated the trade and intercourse laws regulating trade with the Indians, Luján may also have forfeited the one-thousand-dollar bond he had posted to obtain his trading license. The records are silent on this matter, but they show that Luján argued his innocence in the case to New Mexican and federal officials in Washington. Luján went to an Abiquiú friend, Lafayette Head (who would be appointed first Tabeguache Ute agent in Colorado in 1861), and had him write a formal affidavit describing the New Mexican system of fostering Indian children (emphasizing the positive aspects of it, of course). Head himself owned Ute servants and fostered Ute children. This document, along with Luján's version of the Utah trial and his protests that he had obtained children, "but not for slaves," was apparently presented to the superintendent of Indian affairs, James C. Calhoun, and the acting superintendent, John Greiner (who was also the first Ute Indian agent at Taos, 1850–53). Greiner paraphrased parts of this protest in a letter of petition and complaint sent in Luján's behalf to the commissioner of Indian affairs, Luke Lea. Apparently, the New Mexican officials sided with Luján, telling the commissioner that "there is no truth whatever in the [Utah] charges."[1]

That the Indian officials' opinion of Indian servitude coincided with Luján's is not surprising. As previously noted, the wealthy and influential officials of New Mexico—before and after U.S. occupation—were some of the largest "employers" of these slaves/servants. When later Indian agency officials attempted to free these servants, the New Mexico legislature itself formulated a reply in which it, too, argued that "according to ancient custom [Indian captives] have become constituted as adopted children of the persons under whose control they are, and they are treated by them as members of their own legal family, and many of them are as such adopted, and married, and enjoy the same guaranties as the legitimate children."[2]

Whether or not Don Pedro León lost his thousand-dollar bond, he suffered sufficient financial losses that it took several years for him to recover. The extent of his financial problems is apparent in the record of his subsequent visit to Utah in the spring of 1853 as part of the trading caravan of Dr. C. A. W. Bowman, another Abiquiú resident. But unlike in previous years, this time he came as but one of twelve employees—trader and/or guide?—"all Peons."[3] The following year he was working for the government as a member of the New Mexico mounted militia fighting Apaches. From Don Pedro León, the Indian trader had been reduced (temporarily?) to the status of a peon.

## EFFECT IN NEW MEXICO

It is clear from the extant records that the covert sale of Indian children from Utah to New Mexicans continued for a while in spite of the laws. Either New Mexicans traveled surreptitiously into Utah Territory or the Utes took their captives to Colorado and New Mexico themselves. Wákara traveled to the Green River to sell his crop of slaves in 1853 and wintered that year among the Navajos. And Luján was still trading with the Weeminuche Utes (Ute Mountain Utes) in southern Utah-Colorado in 1864. Lafayette Head's 1865 enumeration of Indian slaves in southern Colorado listed eighty-eight in the San Luis Valley, mostly Utes under the age of ten acquired in the 1860s, and sixty-five in Costilla County, mostly obtained from New Mexico. In 1870 Head still had five Indian "servants" living with him and would raise at least two Ute girls in his home, at least one of whom adopted his surname.[4] Catholic church records in New Mexico continued to record Paiute ("Pah-Ute") baptisms, and census records reveal Paiutes living in New Mexico who were born long after the law against Indian slavery and trading in Utah had been passed. Indeed, the 1870 census records for Luján himself reveal the presence of two Paiute boys as part of his household who could not have been born before 1856 and 1859, respectively. And Mormons continued to witness and record Ute slave raiding and trading among the Paiutes, although the practice was dwindling.[5]

But the Indian slave trade did not cease in New Mexico. As the supply of Ute and Paiute captives diminished, there was simply a shift in the pattern of slave gathering and distribution in New Mexico after the mid-1850s.[6] Whereas between 1800 and 1859 the largest number of Indian captives arriving in the northern New Mexico trade centers had been Ute-Paiutes (corresponding with the same period in which trade and alliances with the Utes had increased, particularly along the Old Spanish Trail),[7] after Luján's trial generated the legal machinery to curtail that trade, the number of Navajo captives increased dramatically while the Ute-Paiutes declined. David Brugge remarked on this correlation when he wrote in his study on Navajo captives how, "as a result of Mormon efforts to stop the slave trade in Utah, the northern slave raiders, both white and Ute, took quick advantage of the [Navajo] wars to supply the expanding northern slave markets by raids on the Navajos." In a significant footnote to western history, these slave raiders would play a major part in the ultimate defeat and subjugation of the Navajos.[8]

In any case, the slave trade was doomed to extinction in New Mexico as it had been in Utah when the new American population moved in. Eventually, Americans in New Mexico began to agitate against the ownership of Indian slaves, which was somehow seen as more reprehensible than the institutionalized black slavery of the Old South. As early as 1852 a letter to the editor of the *Santa Fe Weekly Gazette* railed against Indian slavery, writing:

> There is in this country a state of things existing which is much more worthy the efforts of your philanthropists, your Abolitionists and your nigger-loving whites, than the question of slavery; and that is the fact that there are thousands, I might say, of Indian women and children who have been stolen from their families and sold into slavery, worse than *Southern slavery*. . . . They will go out, on the pretense of trading with the Indians, and watch the time when the men are absent, pounce upon the women and children, and take such as they think will sell profitably. . . . Why does not the Commissioner of Indian Affairs look into this matter? or has the "Great *Father*" at Washington forgot that he has any red children in New Mexico?[9]

And in 1853 the same newspaper published excerpts from a Missouri paper that condemned the New Mexicans for instigating war with the Indian, who, after his "Wigwam circle [was] invaded, and his squaws and papooses rifled from him and carried away into slavery, . . . follow[ed] the instincts of nature" and took his "only redress in reprisal—capture for capture—slavery for slavery." "It only proves," went on the editor of this slave-state newspaper, "that *our Christianity* and *civilization*, so far as they *tolerate* such things, are but a very slight improvement upon the barbarism of the ignorant savage."[10]

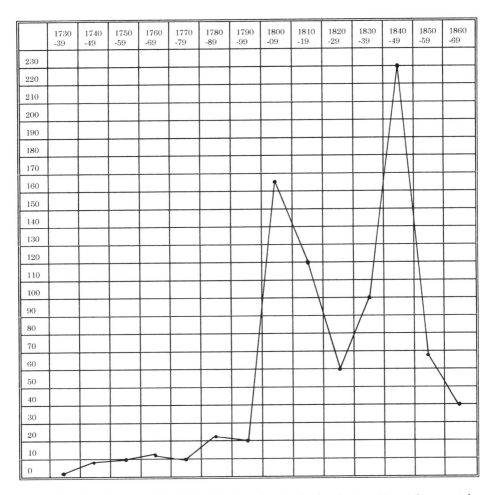

13. *Number of Ute/Paiute captives in New Mexico, 1730–1870, by decade. Some Ute captives were taken in frontier wars in northern New Mexico and account for the numbers between 1730 and 1770. As trade increased after the Rivera (1767) and Dominguez (1776) expeditions, the numbers of captives increased, most dramatically at the turn of the century and again during Chief Wákara's leadership in the 1840s. The numbers of captives drop when Navajo wars supplied captives, in the 1830s and 1860s. Adapted from data in David M. Brugge,* Navajos in the Catholic Church Records of New Mexico, 1694–1875, *Research Report no. 1 (Window Rock, Ariz.: Navajo Tribe Parks and Recreation Department, 1968), frontispiece.*

Indeed, many viewed peonage and debt bondage as even more inhumane than chattel slavery since masters could work their servants through their productive years and then cast them aside without obligation to care for them later as owners did for their black slaves. In 1865 the Thirteenth Amendment would make slavery illegal in the territories, although the "voluntary" servitude of Indians and peons remained legally exempt. In 1865 President Johnson also ordered the trade in

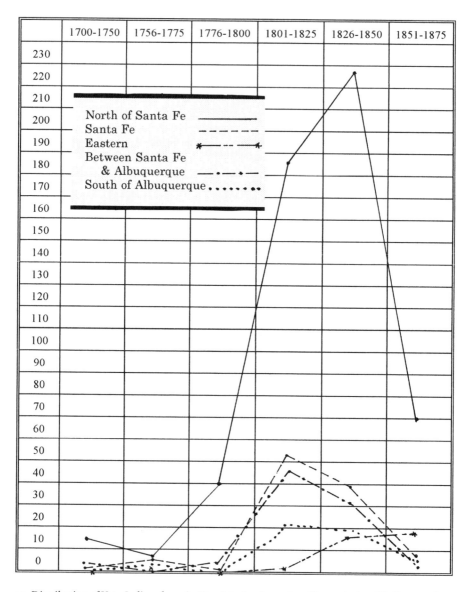

|  | 1700-1750 | 1756-1775 | 1776-1800 | 1801-1825 | 1826-1850 | 1851-1875 |
|---|---|---|---|---|---|---|
| 230 | | | | | | |
| 220 | | | | | | |
| 210 | | | | | | |
| 200 | North of Santa Fe | | | | | |
| 190 | Santa Fe | | | | | |
| 180 | Eastern | | | | | |
| 170 | Between Santa Fe & Albuquerque | | | | | |
| 160 | South of Albuquerque | | | | | |
| 150 | | | | | | |
| 140 | | | | | | |
| 130 | | | | | | |
| 120 | | | | | | |
| 110 | | | | | | |
| 100 | | | | | | |
| 90 | | | | | | |
| 80 | | | | | | |
| 70 | | | | | | |
| 60 | | | | | | |
| 50 | | | | | | |
| 40 | | | | | | |
| 30 | | | | | | |
| 20 | | | | | | |
| 10 | | | | | | |
| 0 | | | | | | |

14. *Distribution of Yuta Indian slaves in New Mexico, by region. The majority of Indian captives remained in the areas to which they were first brought and sold; not unexpectedly, then, most Ute/Paiute captives were found in northern New Mexico. Adapted from data in David M. Brugge,* Navajos in the Catholic Church Records of New Mexico, 1694–1875, *Research Report no. 1 (Window Rock, Ariz.: Navajo Tribe Parks and Recreation Department, 1968), p. 37.*

Indian captives suppressed, and in 1867 Congress passed an act abolishing the system of peonage. The earlier, half-hearted attempts to enforce the antislavery laws were given more teeth in 1867 and 1868, and captives were actively sought out and given their freedom—if they wanted it (which some did not). With these measures, combined with the establishment of controlled Indian reservations and military posts, the trade in new Indian slaves had been curtailed in New Mexico by the end of the 1860s.[11]

A three-hundred-year legacy of forced Indian servitude would grind to a halt within twenty years of American occupation of the Spanish borderlands. What had begun in 1851 at the trial of Pedro León Luján in Mormon-dominated Utah was concluded with the abolition of Indian slavery in Colorado and New Mexico as well.[12]

## EFFECT IN UTAH

The ramifications of the case were especially marked in Utah. Almost immediately on the heels of the Mexicans' trial, the Utah legislature implemented a new act to regulate the acquisition and care of Indian children as part of its program of spiritual and physical redemption of the Indians.[13] Brigham Young told the Utah legislature on January 5, 1852, that he recommended delivering the children that the Indians were "gambling away, selling, and otherwise deposing of," or the prisoners they were "sacrificing," and allowing them to be reared by Mormon settlers. Young went on to assert:

> No person [meaning the Utah Mormons] can purchase them
> without their becoming as free, so far as natural rights are
> concerned, as persons of any other color. . . . It seems indeed that
> any transfer would be to them a relief and a benefit. . . . This may
> be said to present a new feature in the traffic of human beings; it is
> essentially purchasing them into freedom instead of slavery; but it
> is not the low, servile drudgery of Mexican slavery, to which I
> would doom them, not to be raised among beings scarcely
> superior to themselves, but where they could find that
> consideration pertaining not only to civilized, but humane and
> benevolent society.[14]

Young went on to recommend that "in return for favors and expense which may have been incurred on their account, service should be considered due." Thus, it was "necessary that some law should provide the suitable regulation under which all such indebtedness should be defrayed."[15] The legislature answered with an "An Act for the Relief of Indian Slaves and Prisoners," which provided for the indenture of Indian children, its purpose to "extend unto this degraded and down trodden race such relief as can be awarded to them."[16] Shortly thereafter, Brigham Young instructed missionaries going to the southern Utah Indians to obtain as many Indian children as they could as part of their duties.[17]

Many of these children were acquired from parents who traded their children, either through greed for the white man's trade goods—clothing, beads, trinkets, food, and especially cattle, horses, and, for a while, armaments—or because they could not afford to raise the children themselves. Others were purchased from Indian raiders who still trafficked in captives and needed a market. Sometimes the missionaries even arranged for Indians to locate children for them. In May 1854 an Indian addressed elders in Harmony and agreed his band "would try and get some papooses, if not they would be mad but would not fight for them. They would bring these children to us."[18]

Once obtained, the children could be, and not uncommonly were, traded, bartered, or given away to others. Generally, the purchasers of these children recorded that they had acquired them in order to provide them a better life. For example, Jacob Hamblin recorded he purchased a boy in 1854 "that I might let a good man have him that would make him useful." Later the same year he bought three girls so they would not starve. At an 1853 peace parley Brigham Young bought from Wákara two Shoshone children whom he saw unclothed and starving. And the settlers of Parowan bought children from Wákara whom they saw subsisting on grass. All were fed, clothed, and educated to some extent.[19] As ex officio superintendent of Indian affairs for Utah Territory, Young reported to the commissioner of Indian affairs that "very many children are taken into families and have had all the usual facilities for education afforded other children."[20]

That was not completely true. The education of these children, as in New Mexico, consisted mostly of frontier skills. Because Mormons put a higher value on formal education than many New Mexicans, however, some of their Indian children also received some formal studies not unlike those of other children of

15. *Sally Young Kanosh. Courtesy of the Utah State Historical Society.*

the period. But Indian children were seldom treated as equals to their white brothers and sisters. The 1860 census, for example, shows that more than half the Indian
children listed had no formal education at all. In one prominent instance, Sally
Young, the girl acquired by Brigham Young in 1847 and whom he described as having been raised alongside his own children and with the same opportunities, did
not receive the same treatment. She was never taught to read or write like the
Young children, although she became a skilled seamstress, cook, and nanny for the

*16. Nicaagat. Courtesy of the Smithsonian Institution.*

family's other children. Nor did she live among Young's children but remained with the other servants of his house. Ultimately, she accepted the marriage suit of the prominent Pahvant chief and Mormon convert Kanosh, but only after pressure from Young, who urged her repeatedly to accept Kanosh as a good example to the other Indians in his band. She reluctantly left the Young mansion for the somewhat less palatial brush lodge of an Indian. Despite eventually being given a log cabin by her doting husband, she continually pined for her "family" in Great Salt Lake City though the Youngs never again communicated with her.[21]

Foster Indian children raised by the Anglo-Mormon families in Utah did not assimilate as well as their New Mexican counterparts.[22] Many did not survive, having little resistance to the white man's diseases,[23] and few found a place in the Anglo-Mormon community. Brooks reports in her study of fostered children in southern Utah that even when raised by indulgent families, many grew up afraid of Indians, were victims of sarcastic remarks of others, and generally carried a stigma of inferiority.[24]

These fostered Indians did not blend in well with the white community, and intermarriages were rare. Occasionally, women found husbands as a plural wife (often under pressure by a man's ecclesiastical superior)[25] or bore illegitimate mixed-blood children. Men almost never married. One fostered Indian girl declared to a church court: "I have a right to children. No white man will marry me. I cannot live with the Indians. But I can have children, and I will support the children that I have. . . . God meant that a woman have children."[26] Another girl stated on her deathbed that "it had been a mistake for her ever to suppose that she could be a white girl. Indian children, she said, should be left with their own people where they could be happy; when they were raised in white homes they did not belong anywhere."[27]

Although the children taken into foster homes were supposed to be well treated, some abuses still occurred, and indentured children were sometimes raised less as foster children (which was the ideal) than as exploited Indian servants. A notable example was Nicaagat, or Captain Jack. This Gosiute claimed he ran away from his foster Mormon home after having been repeatedly beaten with a buggy whip by his foster mother; he became a leader among the Whiteriver Utes of northern Colorado, was strongly antagonistic toward whites, and would lead the attack on Major T. T. Thornburg's troops in northern Colorado during the infamous Meeker Massacre in 1879.[28]

Only a few Indian children were able to accommodate themselves to Anglo-Mormon society. Between 1877 and 1889 only a dozen fostered Indians entered Mormon temples.[29] The Pahvant chief, Kanosh, married two "fostered" Indian women who continued to participate in local church activities. Most of Kanosh's Pahvants joined the church, turned to agriculture, and successfully fought removal to the Utah Indian reservation in the 1870s.[30] A few other girls found homes as plural wives to Mormon men.

The effort by Utah officials to halt the Indian slave trade was not immediately successful, of course. Although the 1852 trading season was uneventful,[31] the spring of 1853 brought Mormons into direct confrontation with both the Indian traders and ultimately the Indians themselves.

A large company of New Mexican traders arrived in Sanpete Valley in April, determined to revive the slave trade with the Indians.[32] A truculent Dr. C. A. W. Bowman led the traders and peon auxiliaries, one of whom was the financially reduced Pedro León Luján. The caravan had obviously been formed by the disgruntled Mexican traders, and deliberately headed by a non-Mexican, in order to challenge the white, American Mormons. A native of New York and former fur trader, Bowman had lived in New Mexico for some years and was then residing in Luján's home village of Abiquiú.

Mormon records all agree that the trading party, and Bowman in particular, was actively belligerent. The traders made no secret of their presence and indeed sought out Utah officials, to whom they made open threats of forcibly resisting the edicts against the Mexican trade. Bowman cursed one interpreter (Daniel Jones) for "being a Mormon" and boasted that he had "power at his back to use all the Mormons up."

Despite warnings to be "more careful," the buckskin-clad Bowman traveled to Utah Valley, where at Provo he "accosted" Brigham Young "in a very abrupt manner" and acted "in an insulting and threatening manner." Boasting that he had four hundred Mexicans on the Sevier awaiting his orders,[33] Bowman told Young that the traders "feared nothing for law, and would not be restrained from any pursuit which they chose to follow."

Young's response was quick and decisive. To Bowman's rude demand for "a little private conversation" with him, Young gave an abrupt refusal: "I told him I did not hold private interviews with strangers—that if he had anything to communicate he could do so in writing." To Bowman's threats, Young gave a military response. He immediately issued a proclamation declaring that "there is in this territory, a horde of Mexicans, and outlandish men who are infesting the settlements, stirring up the Indians with guns, ammunition, etc., contrary to the laws of this territory," and ordering a thirty-man detachment of the militia under the command of Captain William Wall to head south. The men were to reconnoiter, warn the settlers to be "on guard" against Mexicans or Indians, and "arrest, and keep in close custody, every strolling Mexican party; and those associating with them, and other suspicious persons or parties, that they may encounter and leave them safely guarded" in local settlements. All Mexicans in the territory were to "remain quiet in the settlements, and not to attempt to leave under any consideration, until further advised."[34]

Young proved justified in his fear that the Mexicans might stir up the Indians. Six months later he would note that the Indians who had visited the settlements in the spring and summer of 1853 "manifested a turbulent spirit; and although evidently aiming to conceal it, plainly showed that they had been tampered with, and that their feelings were very different than upon former visits." Wákara was described as "surly in his feelings and expressions," and it was reported that he "has repeatedly endeavored to raise an excitement and open war out of small pretexts."[35]

The new Indian agitation was attributed directly to the Mexican traders. Bowman's traders had hoped to incite the Indians to support them against the Mormon interlopers by telling the Utes that the settlers had not paid them sufficiently for the lands they were usurping and that the Indians had the right to take Mormon cattle as recompense.[36] Such an action was certain to lead to reprisals and open warfare; the traders stood to gain if Indian hostilities drove the Mormons from the land.[37]

Bowman's threats came to nothing, however, and Wall's military expedition met no resistance. Some other Mexicans were harassed or jailed in southern settlements; these complained in exaggerated terms to other travelers that they had been "badly treated by the Mormons," who were "threaten[ing] to shoot or imprison all Americans passing through their country," but their bluster was recognized for what it was, frustration at being thwarted in their Indian slave trade.[38] Bowman's traders were taken into informal custody by Utah officials, and Bowman was subsequently killed by Indians who suspected he had cheated them. Ultimately, the Mexican traders left peacefully.[39]

Young's direct action successfully drove the traders out of Utah—and underground for a while—but heightened Indian hostility. Wákara did not care to whom he sold his human merchandise and felt that Mormons would suffice as well as Mexicans, as long as they were willing to trade him the guns and ammunition he needed.[40] But by fall Utah officials had declared that no arms were to be further traded to the Indians.

Thus, as the trade in Indian children continued to limp along for a while, underground with gentiles and legally with Mormons, the Utah laws on Indian slavery and Mexican trade placed a stranglehold on an old and profitable way of life for the Utes. Their hostility erupted in July 1853 into what has been called the Walker War,[41] a brief but bloody "war" that most Utah historians recognize as having been caused as much by anger over the now-defunct Mexican-Indian slave trade as by encroaching white settlements on Indian land or friction between cultures.[42] Wákara told Americans traveling to California through Utah in 1853 that the Mormons were "fools" for abandoning their homes during the war; his intention was not to drive them out, for then there would be no cattle for him to take[43]—and no market for his captives. Indeed, at the end of the war Wákara asked that the slave trade be resumed as before or with the Mormons absorbing the lost New Mexican trade.[44]

Wákara died of pneumonia within the year, and with his death the Ute side of the trade soon dwindled and died as well.[45]

## CHAPTER SEVEN

# THE TRIAL OF DON PEDRO LEÓN IN RETROSPECT

The trial of Don Pedro León Luján brought to a head the problems of Indian slavery that were plaguing the new Mormon settlers in Utah. The guilty verdict against Luján and his trading party was needed by Utah officials in order to interdict the Mexican trade and so strangle the traffic in Indian slaves. Brigham Young made a show of holding an impartial trial, but the outcome could not have been otherwise. If the trade could not be shown to be illegal, then the Mormons could not keep the traders from "tampering" with the Indians or providing them with the arms they could use against Mormon settlers.[1] The Indians could neither be controlled by the Utah officials nor be persuaded to move to Indian reservations, for with Mexican wealth they remained independent and mobile. Mobility and independence meant there was no need to abandon traditional ways for the agrarian lifestyle the whites saw as "civilized" and productive. And if the trade could not be prevented, the Utes would not stop raiding the impoverished Indians the Mormon elders were trying to convert to Mormonism and agriculture in southern Utah, and, in the northern settlements, the intertribal hostilities against the Shoshones would continue. And, not least of all, there would be no end to the gross inhumanity of the slaver to his captive which Mormons were forced to witness.

It was not that the Mormons objected to slavery per se. Black slavery was a part of life in 1851, and black slaves and their masters, though in a minority, were influential in the new territory. Slavery was at that time an embattled issue in Congress and had been a touchy problem in recent Mormon history as well. The creation of the territory itself had been a part of a compromise over slavery, and Utah would eventually have to take a stand on it. Naturally, the question of slavery became one of the major points of the Pedro León trial itself as the territorial judiciary attempted to sort out the difference between allowing black but prohibiting Indian slavery. After all, some of the confiscated goods of the Mexicans were Indian captives, and the court had to determine if they should be treated (sold) as property. Shortly after the trial the Utah legislature would pass laws prohibiting

Indian slavery but regulating the treatment of black slaves—a tacit acceptance of black slavery in Utah.

And yet, earlier in the spring, Brigham Young had recommended that his people begin acquiring—that is, purchase or barter for—as many Indian children as possible in order to place them in Mormon homes to be raised and acculturated within the Mormon society. As a consequence, Mormon settlers began obtaining as many Indian children as they could, at the same time legally expelling New Mexican traders for doing much the same thing. Luján was undoubtedly right when he insisted he had been refused a license to trade because he was not Mormon. It is a little difficult to see, from a purely legal perspective, what the difference was between a Mormon who took a child in return for an ox that had been killed for food, and a New Mexican who took an Indian child in recompense for a horse that had been similarly slaughtered and eaten. Or the distinction between the selling of children into legal indentures in Utah and the selling of children into unwritten but traditional indentures in New Mexico.

The difference could only come in the perceptions of an expected quality of life for captive Indian children: Mormons believed that they offered foster parents, a home, a true religion, and a superior lifestyle, but that only drudge slavery awaited the Indian children in New Mexico among "beings scarcely superior to themselves." Jacob Hamblin, a Mormon who witnessed the purchase and tearful separation of parents from their children, wrote that he felt heartsick to see them dragged from their homes to become slaves to the gentiles.[2] Mormons were told that through this program only a few generations would pass "ere they [the Indians] should become a white and delightsome people." Brigham Young gave his opinion that "the Lord could not have devised a better plan than to have put us where we [are] in order to accomplish that thing . . . [to] let a remnant of the seed of Joseph be saved."[3]

And yet this was a feeling that simply echoed a policy long enunciated by the Spanish, that captive Indian children raised in foster Hispanic homes (or simply captive Indians) were better off where they could be taught the Christian religion and receive training in farming and domestic skills. Captivity was necessary, and the only practicable method of civilizing wild Indians.[4]

What, then, was the difference between what the Mormons were doing and what Luján and other New Mexicans were doing?[5]

In terms of their captivity, once Indian children were in non-Indian homes, their life differed only in that the culture of Americans and Mexicans differed. In both Mormon and New Mexican homes the Indian children were expected to work alongside the other children. They were fed, clothed, and (theoretically) educated near the level of the children of their captors. Despite Mormon indenture laws requiring Indian children to receive at least three months of formal education per year along with the white children, records indicate that this was not always the case, including in Brigham Young's own home. Indian children in both cultures were treated prejudicially; in neither society was an Indian—educated or not—considered quite equal to a non-Indian.

Although the stigma of enslavement, however temporary, added to the social misfortune of being an Indian in New Mexico, in Utah the prejudice against Indians—just because they were Indians—was actually more pronounced. There were comparatively few Indians, and the distinction between the white-skinned Mormon and the dark-skinned Indian was great.[6] This prejudice created problems for Indians raised in Mormon homes.

What ameliorated things for former Indian captives in New Mexico was the large pool of *genízaros* among whom they could interact and associate. Additionally, the difference in physical traits was not as pronounced, as many of the New Mexicans had a good deal of Indian blood in their veins already. And culturally, on the New Mexican northern frontier, where many of the Indian captives were concentrated, elements of the Indian lifestyle were common. Clothing and survival skills were often drawn from the Indian way of life, and Indians were frequent visitors to the plazas.[7]

But in the clustered settlements of the Mormons, even on the frontier, there was a higher degree of a transplanted Old World society, partly because of the rapid influx of new settlers fresh from the East or from Europe. On the other hand, New Mexican frontier settlements were gradual adaptations of older frontier cultures that had lost much of their European mark in favor of the practical survival arts of the area's original Indian inhabitants.

In one major respect the Mormons differed radically from New Mexicans: the Mormons were never caught up in the slave trade as slave traders themselves, nor did they seek captives strictly for menial service (though once they owned them, they were not averse to working them). Although an Indian child once purchased could be given as a gift, traded, or bartered among Mormons, most were acquired not from slavers but through purchase from the children's parents, who were seeking either to rid themselves of an extra mouth or to find a better home for their children. Sometimes a child was forced on a Mormon by an Indian slave trader. But Mormons themselves, although they were known occasionally to ask Indian friends to acquire children for them, never carried out slave raids to obtain their young converts and laborers as New Mexicans did.

The main reason Mormons purchased young captives was not to fill labor needs[8] but to raise up a "righteous" generation of Indians as a means of temporal and spiritual salvation, as well as to make an end run around the Mexican slavers by intercepting their product. Juanita Brooks believed that nothing short of religious fervor and a strong faith that these children were worth redeeming could have prompted many of the adoptions, because the Indians were often too young at first to work for their keep.[9] Although religious fervor may have motivated most Mormons, the Indians were certainly not too young to be raised as menials. New Mexicans had been doing it for years, and quite profitably, too. And there were undoubtedly some Mormons who did acquire these foster children as cheap laborers, though they were probably in the minority.[10]

How realistic were the Mormon attempts at fostering? Any success at thwarting slavers by purchasing children is doubtful, for it would more likely have only increased the market, creating a greater demand for slaving. The goal of acquiring children to help raise a "righteous" generation of Indians was also naive. In the few decades the Mormons actively practiced Indian indenturing, they could not have purchased enough children to do the job right. It would have taken thousands of homes—and then the very acculturation process would have dislocated the children, leaving them with little influence over their own, nonacculturated people. The removal of Indians to distant reservations soon brought an end to these attempts in any case.

The experiment in Utah of raising a generation of acculturated Indians lasted only a few decades, and those who were fostered generally did not fare well. Acculturated foster children did poorly when they tried to return to wild bands. The acculturation itself had destroyed their identity, as it did in New Mexico. But in New Mexico there was a social mechanism by which these acculturated, detribalized Indians could be absorbed into a viable subculture. In Utah there was not. Brooks's study of fostered Indian children is a doleful tale of dislocated individuals who had no place to go when they left their Mormon families.[11] Had fostering increased its numbers and continued for generations as in New Mexico, a subculture would undoubtedly have developed in Utah as well. But such a group did not exist for these early fostered Indian children.

Nevertheless, this negative assessment of the Mormon experiment is not a vindication of the New Mexican slave trade. Most of the trade was reprehensible. Captives were usually taken violently, and their parents and relatives killed in the raids. Indian captors tended to be callous and brutal, and Mexican traders paraded their human wares as if they were animals. Certainly the practice of enforced servitude for any group of people could never be pleasant. Although there were many instances (particularly on the frontier) in which children became part of the family or preferred the Hispanic life, New Mexico records also tell of numerous cases in which they did not.[12] Older captives were often mistreated, and owners sometimes lied about or hid their Indian servants when American officials sought to free them.[13] When the government proffered freedom to Indian servants, the majority of them in the San Luis Valley accepted it. Certainly the practice of slave trading and raiding perpetuated Indian hostilities and resulted in great loss of life, let alone freedom.

Turning to the trial of Pedro León et al.—how fair was it? According to Daniel Jones, despite "a great deal of prejudice and bitter feelings," Brigham Young did everything he could to see that the traders got a fair trial.[14] They were brought to Great Salt Lake City, where they could be tried before a territorial judge, not a justice of the peace, and a prominent church leader acted as one of their attorneys. The defense attorneys brought up numerous arguments for their clients, often based on technicalities of the law; affidavits and petitions were filed, even after the trial was over, in attempts to gain retrials. When they were found guilty and all their personal goods confiscated to pay the fine, Brigham Young saw to it that they were outfitted with supplies to take them home. Even Luján remarked on Young's kindness in his complaint to the commissioner of Indian affairs.

Nevertheless, it is difficult to see how the Mexicans could have had a fair trial in Utah Territory at that time. In the first place, they were Catholic Mexicans. Although the Mexicans were tried in the new First District Court of Utah Territory, that did not guarantee impartiality. Before the establishment of civil district courts and the appointment of federal judges in September 1850, all judicial questions had been settled in church courts before ecclesiastical leaders; but even after the establishment of civil courts to adjudicate non-Mormon cases or act in criminal actions, the benches continued to be occupied by high Mormon officials and the juries filled by other Mormons. This was particularly true in the winter of 1851–52, when Luján and his compatriots were tried, for the two non-Mormon civil judges had both abandoned their offices a short time before, leaving the Mormon judge, Zerubbabel Snow, as the only authorized justice in Utah. Because Mormons dominated the judicial system, it is not surprising that there were complaints of unfairness from non-Mormons, especially those who had lost their cases.[15]

Added to the handicap of being gentile, the defendants were guilty of being Mexican. Mormons carried the typical nineteenth-century American prejudice against Mexicans. From fur traders on the Missouri to settlers pressing against the Texas and Louisiana borders, Americans usually spoke in denigrating terms of Mexicans with whom they were forced to interact. Brigham Young declared them to be "little better" than the Indians, and another, non-Mormon, traveler in 1846 described Mexicans on the Platte as "swarthy" and "ignoble," with "brutish faces."[16] In 1851 Americans, including a battalion of Mormons that had marched through New Mexico on its return to Utah, had only recently fought a major war against the Mexicans.

Not only were Mexicans of a darker skin in a society and religion that valued lightness of complexion,[17] but they were also Catholic. For many Mormons, as for a majority of Americans whose religious roots reached back to anti-papist England, being Catholic was tantamount to belonging to the church of the devil.[18] It was to this church and its dark-hued, Hispanic society the Mexican traders sought to bring the Indian children. Thus Luján and his trading companions entered the Utah judicial arena with a triple handicap: they were gentile, Catholic, and Mexican.

Add to this set of disadvantages that they were a major cause of the Indian slave trade that was bedeviling the Mormon communities, and it is surprising that they received as open and fair a trial as they did. The Mormon officials, first and last, arrested and tried the traders in an attempt to stop the Indian slave trade. But the Mexican traders were tried not for slave trading—slave trading was legal in the

United States and was still legal in Utah Territory—but only for their infraction of Indian trading laws. This was the sole count on which they could be held, since they had done nothing else that was actually illegal, and the Utah officials had to have something on which they could pin a conviction. The newly extended Trade and Intercourse Act provided that law.

Since the Mexicans had been denied a license by Brigham Young, they could not trade with the Indians. Yet they were found with Indian captives, thereby proving that they had had dealings with the Indians. Therefore, they must have been guilty of trading without a license. Or so the courts reasoned.

Of course, the court instructed the jury that if it determined that the Mexicans had been coerced into their trade, they could not be found guilty, because they had been unwilling partners. But if the jury believed the Mexicans were only trying to cover their actions by claiming this defense—in other words, if the traders were lying about the coercion—then they were guilty. Obviously, the jury believed the traders had lied to cover their "crime," for they found the Mexicans guilty and the fine was assessed.

So why believe the Mexican story? How do we know the traders weren't lying? The answer is, we don't. But in view of the circumstantial evidence, the documented responses, and Ute trading traditions, it is more than likely that they were telling the truth.

There is no question that the Luján company had come to Utah for the specific purpose of trading for Indian children. Not only was it the traditional trade in central Utah and their trade items those typically bartered for children, but they told Brigham Young up front that this was what they had come to trade for. There does not appear to have been anything surreptitious about the expedition. Indeed, Luján was above board in his dealings. When he arrived in Utah with an expired license to trade with the Utes, he made an extended trip to locate Brigham Young in order either to renew his license or to obtain a new one. The wording of court affidavits make it clear that Luján fully expected to receive permission to trade: he had traded for years with the Utes, the trade in captive children was of long standing and an acceptable part of life in New Mexico, and the expiration of his license was a mere technicality that the Utah Indian superintendent could easily remedy.

Luján was probably astounded to be refused a license to trade with the Indians. Nevertheless, following this refusal, he immediately sent the majority of the expedition back to New Mexico while he embarked on a quick trip back to Great Salt Lake City for supplies for the return trip.

The records also indicate that when the Indians first began to raid Luján's camp and steal horses, Mormon officials were informed of it and even aided the Mexicans in their attempts to regain their stock. So the Mormons in Sanpete were aware that the Mexicans were already having problems with the Indians for refusing to trade. It does not seem likely that the Indians would have raided a camp they were planning to trade with; it was not in character for them to antagonize their long-standing trade partners. But it is in character if Luján had refused trade with them. This had been the Indian course of action on previous occasions. There was no logical reason for Luján to remove the remnant of his expedition to the Spanish Fork River on the south end of Utah Valley unless he was trying to avoid the traditional trade rendezvous of the Utes along the Sevier and in Sanpete Valley. In 1853, when Dr. Bowman came to trade, his traders camped on the west side of Sanpete Valley and he came to Utah Valley only to flout his trade in front of Young. Wákara and his kin preferred to remain south of Utah Valley, especially after the development of several Mormon settlements there and because he was at odds with some of the peace-faction chiefs who made the valley their home.[19] Therefore, it is logical to believe that Luján was trying to protect the remnants of his caravan from further attacks by Indians who were angry because he would *not* trade as he had before.

As for the claim that the Mexicans had been coerced into keeping the Indian children as recompense for animals stolen and, in some cases, eaten, it is probably the most believable part of the story. The Mexican traders maintained that all the Indian captives were taken only on the insistence of the Indians in lieu of stolen stock, or were simply thrown at them and the stock taken. It is reminiscent of other stories of Spaniards who traded in Ute country, who either traded for captives or were attacked and/or forced to take them anyway. By 1851—and before the interdiction of the Mexican trade angered the Indians—the Mormons had also been coerced into trading for captive Indian children from the Utes on a number of occasions. Mormon records and diaries relate many stories in which Mormons were forced to take, or sometimes willingly took, Indian children in compensation for animals stolen or weapons demanded.[20]

Thus, the only reason for the members of the all-Mormon jury not to believe the Mexicans' defense must have been that they could not conceive that the

Mexicans were telling the truth or believe that the Mexicans—perhaps any Mexicans, but especially those who would deal in the slave trade—could be honest in their dealings. One of the jurors himself stated to the prosecuting attorney, *before* the trial, that the Mexicans were guilty because they had Indian captives in their possession and *that was all the evidence he needed.*[21]

In today's courts the trial would have been declared a mistrial, at the very least because of the evidence of pretrial prejudice of the jury and of a juror consorting with the prosecuting attorney before the trial. Indeed, the Mexicans' attorneys filed a motion for retrial based on this irregularity, but the petition was denied, as was every other petition for retrial. Eventually, Brigham Young simply referred the Mexicans to the commissioner of Indian affairs and closed the courts to further Mexican appeals.

Did the attorneys for the Mexicans try their best to get an acquittal for their clients, or were they part of a Mormon "conspiracy" to indict them? Again, there is nothing to prove that the lawyers were not doing their best to defend their clients. The Mexicans' attorney in Manti, Andrew Siler, wrote several letters to the Salt Lake attorney, G. A. Smith, offering advice on their defense and insisting that he wanted the men to receive a just trial. Based on what records are available, it appears that the attorneys tried to defend their clients as well as they could. Certainly the flurry of special motions and petitions for retrial or redress that they continued to file with the court after the trial was over and during the hearings on the libel and petition of debt is indicative of their continuing attempts to serve the Mexicans. Also, as shown in the arguments that were made in the case and on which the court commented in its published findings, the attorneys brought up a variety of arguments to get around the accusation of trading "in Indian country."

Despite the numerous technicalities on which the case seems to have been based, however, the only defense the traders really had was that they were coerced into accepting the Indian captives. On this hung their innocence or guilt, yet the published court "Information" spent little time discussing this question. The prosecution certainly attempted to prove that they had traded voluntarily, using both the Indian trader, Arapeen, and the Spanish and Indian interpreters as witnesses. It is also clear that there was some concern by the defense that Arapeen's evidence was tainted; Smith and Slayton were probably following Siler's advice when they tried to fight its admissibility. Siler, the Mexicans' Manti attorney, was definitely worried that the Indian testimony was being influenced and perhaps even coached. Certain Indians had already been shown to lie about the trade: Arapeen himself had boasted of trading for a Spanish horse that was actually one of those confiscated from the Mexicans and had been stolen from the court corral!

Arapeen's testimony was not recorded, however, and his evidence must be left to conjecture. It is clear that Siler expected any Indian witnesses to perjure themselves and testify that the Mexicans had traded voluntarily. And it is hard to imagine their testifying to the coercive actions the Mexicans accused them of since they could only have incriminated themselves, not to mention losing the possible gain (reacquisition of the captives) they may erroneously have thought or been led to believe they might make if the Mexicans lost the trial.

Another indication of Luján's "innocence" was his behavior after the trial. Luján didn't act like someone who had been caught trying to subvert the law. On the contrary, his actions are those of a man frustrated with a miscarriage of justice. In Utah he made numerous appeals for retrial, and back in New Mexico he continued his attempts to find judicial redress for his grievances. In Utah he had waived his ownership rights to the Indian captives, which by themselves constituted a major investment, in lost stock if nothing else. In any case, the court found the Indians not to be property, so they could not be sold to pay the five-hundred-dollar fine assessed Luján. In order to meet the fine, then, all the traders' other belongings were sold, and they lost that property as well. On top of these losses was the indignity of having to make their way home on a dangerous trek across the mountains in midwinter, on foot, their food supplied only through the charity of the Mormons who had confiscated their property in the first place.

The arguments Luján made do not sound as if he felt he had done anything wrong; perhaps like others of his time in New Mexico, he felt justified in his trade—at least he used the time-honored arguments for Indian servitude in New Mexico to defend what he was doing. There is no question that the trial involved a clash in cultural values: the Mexicans were unable to see that what they were doing was wrong, and the Mormons were unable to see why the Mexicans couldn't understand that what they were doing was wrong.

Certainly the traders became embittered. A year later Luján returned in the company of other Mexican traders under the direction of a very white Anglo-American, Dr. C. A. W. Bowman, probably as a guide and informant. This time they were belligerent and antagonistic, openly defying the Mormons to try to stop them from trading with the Indians. There was no seeking official permission to trade, simply a blustering statement of intent given in an obvious attempt to provoke trouble.[22] Simultaneously, there was a deliberate effort to poison the minds of the Indians against the Mormons in order to instigate hostilities. Whereas Luján's traders in 1851 brought horses to trade for captives—stock, tack, and buckskins were the only things confiscated (besides the captives)—arms and munitions were specifically mentioned as trade items in Dr. Bowman's 1853 expedition.

If the Mexicans thought they could drive the Mormons out with Indian help, however, they were mistaken, and the Mexican-Indian revolt died before it was born. Only residual bitterness remained to spark the expensive, but unsuccessful, uprising by the Indians in the Walker War a few months later.

Luján may again have found himself in the custody of the Manti officials, but the traders were soon released and left without argument after Bowman died at the hands of Indians.[23] Local police action against other traders discouraged future like incidents.

Unfortunately, the two incidents—Luján's peaceful but ill-fated expedition in 1851 and the provocation of the belligerent traders of 1853—have become fused in the collective historical memory of Utahns. The arrest and trial of Don Pedro León and his companions has been justified not only in terms of stopping the slave trade but in terms of retaliating against Mexicans who defied Utah laws and incited Indians against Mormon settlers.[24] Yet the belligerence of the traders did not cause the trial; on the contrary, it was caused *by* the trial.

As a result of the trial, Utah officials were able to set the precedent necessary to police the Indian trade, interdict the Mexican traders specifically, and determine the illegality of Indian slavery. The Utah legislature subsequently passed laws to regulate the indenturing of Indian children, an act some historians have interpreted as legalizing Indian slavery. Many of these children were victims of the continuing slave trade, but many more were sought out and purchased directly from their parents. Such regulations were necessary to control the treatment of the Indian children, as well as to make it legally clear that these children were not slaves (despite having been purchased or bartered for) so that the non-Mormon trade could be curtailed.

Another interesting effect of the trial was the determination of the legality of black slavery. The legislature shortly thereafter passed laws regulating the treatment of these slaves as well, thus making Utah an unexpected "slave" territory. When New Mexico and Utah were made territories as part of the Compromise of 1850, most people expected Utah to take a position against slavery and believed New Mexico would eventually enter as slave because of its long tradition of peonage and Indian slavery. Although neither territory took the opportunity to vote officially on the issue, interim legislation revealed each one's stance: New Mexico lawmakers wrote memorials against slavery as early as 1848 and would have banned it in their proposed 1850 constitution, whereas Utah officials early on passed laws to regulate both slavery and the treatment of the slaves they acknowledged existed in their territory. Although New Mexico would ultimately accept the extension of slavery through the Dred Scott decision and would write its own slave codes in 1859, only Utah Territory, of all the states and territories in the West, had slave schedules as part of its 1850 and 1860 census rolls, and only Utah ever enumerated black slaves among its population.

Judge Snow also made a significant decision when he determined that the Trade and Intercourse Act of 1834 was intended to regulate trade with Indian tribes when applied to Indians outside Indian territory. Thus settlement in Utah, as well as trade and missionary work, could legally continue among the Indians without infringing on the Trade and Intercourse Act and despite not having extinguished the Indians' title to the land. (It is interesting to speculate if that is why there was no rush to compensate Indians for their lands in Utah; these land claims were not settled until the mid-1940s.)

Snow could hardly have found otherwise without endangering the status of Anglo settlements; no nineteenth-century judge could have. Yet he left open the right for officials to regulate who could traffic with the Indians. Undesirables (apparently this included Mexicans) could not trade, whereas Mormons could. Such a decision, however, left unresolved the question of who was to judge a trader's desirability. A few years later a non-Mormon Indian agent, Garland Hurt, would charge that it was the *Mormons* who were the undesirable traders who were tampering with the Indians and stirring them up against the federal government.

The end of the institutionalized Indian slave trade began with the trial of Pedro León Luján and died two decades later, a victim of a rapidly changing society.

Armed with its newly defined laws and regulations, Utah was able to enforce its ban on Indian slave trading as well as the general Mexican trade on the Old Spanish Trail. Within a short time the explosion of the American population in California and the influx of American emigrants on the Spanish Trail changed the nature and necessity of trade on that route, and the great Mexican trade caravans became a thing of the past.

An additional factor in the decline of the slave trade in Utah was the death of Wákara, the moving genius behind his band of central Utah warriors. His successors were not only hampered by the Mormon laws against slaving but lacked his leadership ability. As the encroachment of white settlements ever more dislocated the Utes and interfered with their traditional way of life, it also broke up their hunting of human prey.

Meanwhile, in New Mexico the increased raiding among Navajos, turned to at first to replace lost Paiute captives, escalated hostilities on that front and obviated the necessity of sneaking captives out of Utah and into New Mexico. Eventually, with the growth of American agitation against Indian slavery in New Mexico, coupled with the confining of Indians on reservations guarded by the military, the trade in Indian captives disappeared, to be replaced by different institutions of labor.

The Indian slave trade ended with the influx of Americans into the Spanish borderlands. Its demise was heralded by the politically necessary trial of Pedro León Luján and completed within twenty years, buried under a flurry of laws against enforced labor and the destruction and corralling of "wild" tribes from whom captives could be harvested.

## Appendix A
# NEW MEXICAN TRADE LICENSES

A copy of the trading license of Pedro Léon is attached to the testimony of Brigham Young, *United States v. Pedro León et al.*, 1st District Court, Doc. 1533, Utah State Archives, Salt Lake City, 13.

---

Territory of New Mexico )

)

County of Santa Fe )

Pedro Leon, has this 14th day of August 1851, entered into a Trade Bond of one thousand Dollars, with approved sureties therto, to comply with and cause his aids, assistants, and servants to comply with all the rules and regulations adopted or that may be adopted by authority of the United States for the regulation of trade and intercourse with all the savage Indian Tribes under the Jurisdiction of said United States in his contemplated trading expedition to the Utah Indians, The said Pedro Leon is therefore authorized to proceed to the Utah Nation of Indians, and trade with them, and with them only in their own localities, and on no other than his own private and individual account.

The authority to trade under this license will expire on the 14th (fourteenth) day of November 1851, but may be revoked at an earlier day.

Santa Fe, August 14th 1851

James C. Calhoun
Superintendent of Indian Affairs

Attest
D. V. Whiting

A copy of this blank trading license is in the Brigham Young Collection, box 47, fd. 36, LDS Church History Archives, Salt Lake City.

---

Copy of a license given to _____ by J. S. Calhoun for trading with the Indians of Utah Territory.[2]

> Executive Department
> Santa Fe, New Mexico
> July 30th, 1851

has this day given his bond, with approved Securities, to observe all the laws and regulations made, or which shall be made, for the government of trade and intercourse with the Indian tribes, and in no respect to violate the same, he is authorized to proceed to the Salt Lake country, in the Territory of Utah for the purpose of trading in said country, and in no other place, and with no other than Utah Indians — and this license will continue in force for six months, if not sooner revoked.

> J. S. Calhoun
> Supt. Ind. Affs.

A copy of the trading license of C. A. W. Bowman is in the Brigham Young Collection, box 47, fd. 36, LDS Church History Archives, Salt Lake City.

Jan. 22, 1853

---

Be it known that, C. A. W. Bowman, Resident of Abiquiu, County of Rio Arriba, having filed his application before me for a license to trade with the Utahs tribe of Indians at the following named places within the boundaries of the country occupied by the said tribe viz Sierra Lanterna between Grand & Green Rivers == and having executed and filed with me a bond in the penal sum of one thousand dollars with Preston Beck

as sureties, conditioned as required by law, for the faithful observance of all the laws and regulations provided for the government of trade and intercourse with the Indian tribes, and reposing special trust and confidence in the patriotism, humanity, and correct business habits of the said applicant, and being satisfied that he is a citizen of the United States as required by law he is hereby authorized to carry on the business of trading with the said Utah Tribe of Indians, at the above named place, for the term of 6 months from the date hereof, and to keep in his employ the following named persons, or any of them in the capacities to their name respectively, viz, Francisco Lopez, Tomas T. Valdez, Jose M. Suaso, Salvador Valdez, Manuel Lonata, Pedro Leon, Musalinia Rito, Jesus M. Suaso, Juan A. Salazar, Jose M. Salazar, Tomas Lucero, all Peons.

All of which persons I am satisfied from my own knowledge or from the testimonials which have been placed in my hands sustain a fair character, and are fit to be in the Indian country.

> Given under my hand and
> Seal this 22nd day of January A.D. 1853
> John Greiner
> for Gov. Lane Supt. Ind. Aff.

Attest
John Ward

# APPENDIX B
## COURT AFFIDAVITS

"Testimony of Brigham Young," in *United States v. Pedro León et al.*, 1st District Court, Doc. 1533 (microfiche), Utah State Archives, Salt Lake City, 11–14.

Gov. B. Young

Testimony in the case of Libel, U.S. v. P. Leon

---

Governor Brigham Young appeared before me in open Court, and testified as follows.

When on my return from the South, the first day of November 1851, I arrived at the City of Manti, in San Pete County, I there found a company of Spanish traders. The Captain of the company, Pedro Leon, presented me with a license, purporting to be signed by J. C. Calhoun, the Superintendent of Indian affairs in New Mexico. I caused a copy of the said license to be taken which I here present to the court, and which is the same I caused to be taken from the original. (No objection urged by counsel to the same.)

Pedro Leon requested a license from me to trade with the Indians. I refused to give him one and gave him the reason that they had come to this place with the express purpose to trade for Indian children to take to New Mexico. I wrote the Governor of New Mexico a letter and gave it to Pedro Leon. He agreed to return immediately to Santa Fe and deliver the letter.

The company as far as I could learn, was employed by this Pedro Leon, as Clerks, servants, traders etc. There not being a good Spanish Interpreter found, it was difficult to find out the real design, or extent of their mission, but this I learned, they wished to trade for Indian children to take to New Mexico. I told them they were at liberty to trade with the whites, but must not trade with the Indians, for the reason that they could not without violating the Intercourse Laws of the United States with the Indians. I judged there were about twenty men in the company of the traders.

Question.   Are the Indians in San Pete, Utah?

Answer.   They are.

Q.   Do you consider Indians property in this Territory?

Ans.   No more than the whites.

Q.   Did the Spaniards, or any portion of them return immediately?

Ans.   When I refused the license to Pedro Leon, he agreed to return to New Mexico.

| | |
|---|---|
| Ques. | Did they return, or any portion of them? |
| Ans. | I do not know that any of the company did return, But understood a portion of them returned in eight or Ten days after I saw them in San Pete. |
| Ques. | Do you know of Indian children having been bought by white people in this Territory? |
| Ans. | I do. |
| Ques. | For what purpose? |
| Ans. | All the Indians that have been bought by the citizens have been bought to obtain their liberty And to save them from starvation, abuse and even death. |
| Ques. by the Court. | Do you, since you resided in this Territory, Know of the Indians trading with Indians, or with the Spaniards, for their children? |
| Ans. | I have known of the Indians trading for Indian children. It is a common practice with them, and according to the best information I can get from the traders among them, they are in the habit of stealing children and selling them. There is an Indian in this Territory by the name of Baptiste, he has followed the business ever since I have resided in this Territory, of trading for Indian children. When he cannot trade for them, he steals them, and takes them to New Mexico and sells them to the Navaho's or Spaniards. This is according to his own and other's statements. |

In the fall of 1847, after we came in here, he, Batiste, brought in our Fort, a young Indian boy and Squaw, that he had stolen in Beaver Valley, from a tribe called the Pi-Band; the boy was about 16 years old and the girl about 18, as near as we could judge. He offered them for sale. The people refused to buy them. Batiste then told the whites if they would not buy them he should kill them. The whites, not believing his statement, still refused to purchase them. Batiste then took out his two prisoners to his camp, and killed the boy. He then returned to the Fort with the girl and offered her for sale. A young man by the name of Charles Decker (a son-in-law of mine) gave Batiste a gun for the girl. She has lived in my family ever since, has fared as my children and is as free.

It is customary with the bands of Indians in this Territory to steal from other bands, their children and Squaws, and if accidents or misfortune, comes upon the Bands holding the slaves, as the death of one of their tribe, in their bands, or other striking circumstances, for them to take a prisoner, and kill him, to appease the wrath of the enemy.

Indian Walker has been in the habit for years of trafficking in Indians. He has never been here with his Band, without having a quantity of Indian children, as slaves. He offers them for sale, and when he has an offer that satisfies him in the price he sells them; and when he cannot get what he thinks they are worth, he says he will take them to the Navaho Indians or Spaniards, and sell them, or kill them, which I understand he frequently does.

I have seen Walkers slaves so emaciated, they were not able to stand upon their feet. He is in the habit of tying them out from their camps at night, naked and destitute of food unless it is so cold, he apprehends they will freeze to death. In that case he will give them something to sleep on, lest he should lose them. This is the general character of the Utah Indians.

There are many other circumstances of a like character which I could relate, but if the Court please I will forbear.

"Testimony of Isaac Morley," January 15, 1852, in First Judicial Court, "Minutes," Utah State Archives, Salt Lake City, 47–48.

Isaac Morley testified as follows, viz. Don Pedro Leon & others in the Valley of San Pete, saw them there, at the time the Governor was there, heard the Governor tell them they must not trade or Traffick in Indian Children, and he forbid it. Understood they came from Santa Fe, understood they came for the purpose of trading Horses for Indian Children.

The Spaniards had near one hundred Horses & mules to trade with the Indians. I counted them myself, saw no other property they had to trade. Do not know from my personal knowledge that they traded for any Children. These Spaniards speak the Spanish Language, & that I do not understand. There was a Court of Inquiry held at the City of Manti in San Pete Valley, and I was present at that court. The Spaniards, I have seen about here, are the same men I saw in San Pete. They are the same men that were brought into here by a writ from this Court in the custody of the Marshall. They had Indian Children with them. Pedro Leon & those arraigned with him, had no Indian Children with them when they came to San Pete to my knowledge. I know the fact that they were arrested by Mr. Peacock, and brought into the Court of Inquiry, But do not know where Mr. Peacock arrested them.

Cross Examined. Manti is the County seat of San Pete County. It was Justices of the Peace that comprised the Court of Inquiry & Heard Mr. Peacock say they had Indian Children with them at the time he arrested them.

The whites at San Pete trade with the Indians, have been counselled so to do by the Governor Before the Territorial organization to purchase Indian Children to save them from misery, starvation, cruelty and death. Don't know how many Indian children the whites have purchased of the Indians. All that have been purchased, have been purchased to make them free. Do not know from my own knowledge that the Spaniards had traded for any children, or had any in their possession. Only there were Indian Children with them; when the officer brought them into the Court of Inquiry.

I Certify the foregoing   )

to be correct     )

"Deposition of Phillipe Santiago Archuleta," in *United States v. Pedro León et al.*, 1st District Court, Doc. 1533 (microfiche), Utah State Archives, Salt Lake City, 325–330.

|  |  |
|---|---|
| U.S. | Deposition of Phillipe Santiago Archuleta |
| vs. | and Y. A. Pomeroy [Lujan testimony] |
| Pedro Leon et al. | Taken Jan. 16, 1852 |

Phillipe Santiago Archuleta
Testimony in case of libel

Lives in Taos, in New Mexico. Came here with his uncle Miguel Archuleta, came into this valley in October last but don't know what his uncle came for, his uncle knows what he came here for, and came because his uncle wanted him to come. He and his uncle did not come alone, but they came with them. There was twenty eight in all in the company; twenty one [illegible] property being on their own account and residue of them hired servants. Heard of Pedro Leon before he left New Mexico, and been acquainted with him when they left for the valley. Knows the following named persons who have presented their claims: Pedro Leon, Jose Manuel Sena, Alijio Bicente Chaves, Manuel Archuleta, Johns. Antonio Baldineros, Jn. Albino Mestes, Miguel Archuleta. These persons are in and about Salt Lake City except Manuel Archuleta—all these were in the company of the twenty eight last mentioned. Ques. of the Court: hearing of that company of twenty-eight any goods when they left Taos [illegible]

Ans. What I brought myself I remember but others I do not—we came on horses and mules. Does not know how many horses and mules they had, had a good many, but [illegible] the numbers. Every man had an animal to ride and others to pack. Had flour and provisions on the other horses, and some other things.—Packed goods for his uncle. Pack had bread and flour, [illegible] and blankets and shirts. Traded these goods with the Utahs for horses and buckskins, sold the buckskins in this place, some of the horses were also sold here. Some were stolen and others sent to Santa Fe. Done their trading on the other side of the Rio Grande. He and his uncle traded their goods there, and saw others there trading. Saw some of these 8 men that had put in their claims here. After [illegible] River Quatz. Two days travel beyond the Rio Grande. When the company left that river they started to come here to this city to trade. Had a license to trade with the Ute Indians and did not know any thing about a line. The officer that gave them the license in New Mexico gave them permission to trade with the Utah Indians, he did not know there was any line in the Territories to restrict him from going anywhere. Do not know of any license except in the company and that was given to the captain of the company Pedro Leon. Came here to sell his animals [illegible, creased] and if that was good to trade with the whites and Indians also, and if the license was not good, to endeavor to get one from the Governor and when the Governor refused them a license they refused to trade with the Indians. Some of the horses they brought here was sold, others was stolen and some were sent back to Santa Fe. Six horses were stole first at San Pete Valley. Utahs were the ones they supposed stole them. States [illegible] never got these horses. Indian Agent at San Pete told Geo. Bean to go and get the horses and mules from the Indians and return [illegible] them to the Spaniards, but they never recovered them. When the company was on the Spanish Fork, they had four horses and two mules stolen likewise. Some of the company went to look for the lost horses and Mules stolen, not any of the horses but saw their skins of two. The horses had been eaten up. Got no pay for them except one squaw. Did not see the trade himself, but said the company had taken the squaw for the two horses that had been eaten up.

The two horses that were eaten belonged to Bisente Chaves he received the squaw and he is one of the party here. Witness was at Salt Creek, band was ahead of him. Witness was with Pedro Leon and Company when they were arrested—was this side (south) of Salt Creek in San Pete Valley about half days travel from Manti City. Jos. A. Baldineros and Bishant Chaves was going on ahead with Mules. Jose Manuel Senyo and Miguel Archuleta were with camp—Witness and the other three were together, don't know how far from the camp might be perhaps 6 or nine miles. Has Indian Children with them. Said Arapeen the Indian had brought and throwed down and took the Spaniard's horses in that place. His uncle was in leanto. Witness was with his uncle. Reports Arapeen caught five horses belonging to his uncle and threw down two Indian children and said if he had a mood to trade he would trade and if he had not he would trade any how. Another Indian catched one of Albino Mestes horses and threw down an Indian child, and rode off with the horse, which makes three Indian children. Witness knows of seven Indians being with the camp, six children and one squaw. [illegible] had Salt Creek, Sevier River. Witness saw hides of horses that had belonged to his uncle and since that time his uncle received an Indian girl of the Indians for the horses eaten. Then followed in the tracks of their animals to Sevier River and they found Indians and charged them with stealing their horses. Indians denied having the horses. Spaniards told them they had followed their tracks right there and they knew they had them. They demanded pay for them. After a while the Indians acknowledged they had the horses. The Indians gave them an Indian Boy and Indian girl for the horses stolen. Said that Leon told the Indians that he did not want their children but wanted their horses to go home with. No other way to get pay for their horses therefore they took them.

Quest. By District Attorney. Indian children bought and sold in New Mexico there is certain men in New Mexico that have Indians to work for them [illegible] and likely to go and work for who they please. But knows nothing of their being slaves. By the court, have any of this company present been in the habit of coming to this country, and trade for Indians, children [illegible].

Answer. Do not know of any one himself, but he has been told the Spaniards of New Mexico had come here and traded for Indian children. Witness himself came a few years ago with a company and traded for Indian children.

Ques. by D.A. Did not these claimants come here to trade with the Indians for Indian children. This objected to by of. of C. Granted by the court.

Ans. That is not possible for him to know [illegible] what they intended to trade but he supposed they came to trade for any thing they could trade for.

Says he heard some of the company say that Jse [illegible] came here to trade for Indian children or anything else he could trade. Had property at the time of their arrest at South Salt Creek, lost Mules & Horses. Had seven Horses and ten Mules. Six of the horses and four Mules are the same that the Marshall has under arrest at Presant.

Cross exam by Def Counsel

Had a horse taken at Sanpete belonging to Antonio Beldineros by the Alcalde [illegible] and given to Arapeen for an Indian Boy. If not been arrested intended to have returned to Santa Fe this fall. Don't know how far from San Pete to Santa Fe, but took them two months to come from Santa Fe to San Pete. He could go alone with their own mules if he wished to go quick, two would do if he wanted to go slow, and take his time. Had no horses of his own when the Marshall arrested except those stated. At the time the other company started back had twenty horses & mules. Company that started back took all the goods and animals. Only left them enough to hunt their animals, and provision to last them until they overtake the camp.

And further saith not.

F. M. Pomeroy. Says and Testifies, saw the Spaniards present all except one about the 12 or 13th of December last staid at his house in this city. They are all claimants here in the suit except one. Spaniards told him they came here in purpose to trade with the whites and get him (witness) to go and interpret for them to trade with [illegible] two animals of them also some skins. When they left here they told me they intended to go direct to Santa Fe. Pedro told witness that he had a license to conduct trade in company with these others he had left the party six (?) days previous to their arriving in San Pete Valley and came up in advance to find the Governor and exhibit to him his license, came on as far as the Provo where a man told him the Governor was down at Iron County. He turned around and proceeded as far as the Sevier River. There an Indian told him the Governor had gone up to San Pete. Pedro arrived at San Pete [illegible] Men [illegible], said he presented the license to the governor. The governor told him that license was not good to trade here. He then asked the Governor to give him another which the Governor refused, and that the Governor [illegible] to go home, but gave him liberty to trade with the whites that he came down here [Great Salt Lake City] and traded in order to obtain his supplies to return home. When he started from here to go home, arriving at Spanish Fork where he left the portion of the company when he came down here, he there heard that three nights previous the Indians had stolen six of their animals, 4 horses and 2 mules. He then directed the company to Pack up and start for Santa Fe except those present here. They were to tarry and hunt up the animals stolen. He, Pedro, would also stay and help hunt the animals then go and overtake the camp. [illegible] ago at Manti. The company that started for Santa Fe took the ~~Santa Fe Road~~ Spanish Fork Road. The remainder who tarried to find their horses took a [illegible] Route, as it came into San Pete Valley at the south Edge.

# CHRONOLOGY OF COMPULSORY
## INDIAN LABOR LAWS IN NEW SPAIN, MEXICO,
## AND THE UNITED STATES

*1452:* Pope Nicholas V decrees that the king of Portugal may "sell into slavery all heathens and 'foes of Christ'" (referring specifically to Moslems). Other popes interpret this to mean all captives of religious wars.

*Early 1500s, by 1526:* Slavery (meaning chattel property, without rights) is forbidden by Spanish law. Nevertheless, the governor of New Mexico is still organizing slave raids against Plains Indians in the early 1600s and using forced labor on building projects.

*Mid-1500s:* Compulsory Indian labor in mines is abolished (but the ban is disregarded on the frontiers of New Spain).

*1548:* Spain passes laws to end Indian slavery in its American dominions, although enforcement of the laws is ineffectual.

*1549:* The encomienda is forbidden; however, Don Juan de Oñate will distribute encomiendas in the early 1600s after his *entrada* into New Mexico, and Don Diego de la Vargas will be offered (but never receive) an encomienda for his accomplishments in the *Reconquista* of New Mexico in 1693.

*1589:* Spain passes Indian labor laws explicitly forbidding chattel slavery and the exploitation of natives.

*Late 1500s:* The continuation of slave raids through north-central Mexico for Indian mine laborers leads to a 1601–2 rebellion.

*After 1618:* War captives, as a punitive measure, can be assigned labor for a specified period of time but cannot be legally sold or bartered.

*Mid-1600s:* Slave raids continue against the Apaches and Utes, along with illegal trade with the Plains Indians. Governor Luis de Rosas uses large numbers of Indian slaves in his personal workshops.

*1680:* Pueblo Revolt, in part a reaction to forced Indian servitude, drives Spaniards from the upper Río Grande.

*1684*: Louis XIV orders Indian (Iroquois) captives to work in French galleys because they are "vigorous and strong and accustomed to strong work" but finds that it creates too much friction between French traders and the Indians, so the captives are returned. This is the only instance of a demand by a home government for Indian labor (usually the demand derived from personal enterprises).

An attempt is made to emancipate Indian slaves in French Louisiana, but it is ineffectual and is abandoned by 1794.

*By 1706*: Spanish officials become a prime outlet for slaves, horses, weapons, and loot from tribes on the Missouri and Platte Rivers.

*1778*: Proclamation issued September 13 prohibits unlicensed trade with the Indians in an attempt to control the flow of contraband to border tribes. The law is ignored.

*By 1812*: Law are passed prohibiting the purchase or trade in captives from the Ute Indians, but frontier commerce between Mexicans and Indians in horses, guns, and captives continues.

*1824*: California provincial governor issues a decree on July 13 forbidding the trade in Indian captives.

*1848*: Memorial passed in New Mexico forbids black slavery.

*1850*: Prospective New Mexican constitution bans black slavery.

*1851–52*: Utah passes legislation recognizing and regulating black slavery but forbidding Indian slavery.

*1865*: Thirteenth Amendment emancipates all slaves in the United States. Indian "indentures" and peons are excluded because they are considered "voluntary" contractual labor.

President Andrew Johnson orders the suppression of the slave trade in Indian captives.

*1865–70*: Indian captives are actively sought out in Colorado and New Mexico in order to emancipate them.

*1867*: Peonage is abolished in New Mexico on March 2.

# NOTES

1. Warren A. Beck, "New Mexico and the Sectional Controversy," in *New Mexico: A History of Four Centuries* (Norman: University of Oklahoma Press, 1962, 1969), 139.

2. Beck, "Sectional Controversy," 145–146.

3. The Indians in the valley were Cumumbahs, who considered themselves Shoshone, not Ute, although they probably had a sizable mixture of Ute blood. Utes could enter the valley unmolested for trade.

4. Title to Indian lands in Utah was never officially extinguished in the nineteenth century; a Ute reservation was established by presidential proclamation in 1863, Indians were enticed there in 1865, and many more fled there during the disastrous Black Hawk War, 1865–73. The land was never "purchased" from them, however, until the settlement of the Land Claims Case for the Confederated Ute Nation in 1948. See Floyd A. O'Neil, "A History of the Ute Indians until 1890," Ph.D. diss., University of Utah, Salt Lake City, 1973; and Floyd A. O'Neil and Kathryn L. MacKay, *A History of the Uintah-Ouray Ute Lands*, American West Center Occasional Papers (Salt Lake City: University of Utah Press, n.d.).

5. On New Mexican slavery and the question of Indian captive status, see Chap. 3.

6. Court documents consistently refer to the traders as Spanish (despite the successful Mexican revolution in 1821), whereas other documents and most historians refer to them as Mexican; following the annexation of New Mexico by the United States, however, they had all become American citizens and are more properly called New Mexicans. Nevertheless, to remain consistent with most historical references, I generally refer to them here as Mexican traders.

7. Pedro León Luján most commonly went by the name Pedro León; this is how he is referred to on his trading license and in the court documents and other contemporary records in Utah. Records from New Mexico indicate that his full name was Pedro León Luján and that he was a well-known Indian trader and military commander from northern New Mexico. The Spanish honorific *Don*—a title that was used in conjunction with his name in some documents—was generally used only with a man's first name(s) and may be the reason Luján so frequently appears with only his first names used. Because Utah history knows him as Pedro León rather than Luján, references within this work—especially those having to do with the Utah "incident," "affair," or case—simply refer to Pedro León rather than the more accurate Luján.

## chapter ONE. The Evolution of a Stereotype

1. In some cases, books on Utah history have ignored the incident entirely. For example, a short book on Utah published in the 1922 "See America First" series

contained only one brief but blatantly paternalistic paragraph about Indian affairs in Utah and nothing at all about the Pedro León incident: "In time there were conflicts between the settlers and the Indians, and then came an Indian War, in which, of course, the Indians were defeated and shown the folly of fighting against the white man, even though it were in defense of their own rights." George Wharton James, *Utah: The Land of Blossoming Valleys* (Boston: Page, 1922), 109. A similar disinterest in early Utah Indian affairs seems to be relegating the incident not simply to footnotes now but out of history texts entirely.

2. Brigham Young Manuscript History, 1853–62 (microfilm) (hereinafter BYMH), Historical Archives of the Church of Jesus Christ of Latter-day Saints, Salt Lake City (hereinafter LDS Historical Archives); *Journal History of the Church*, LDS Historical Archives; *Deseret News Weekly*, Salt Lake City.

3. *El Siglo Diez y Nueve*, July 16, 1853, Mexico. Only one newspaper was being published in New Mexico in 1851–52, the *Santa Fe Weekly Gazette*, but most of its spring–summer issues were not preserved, and subsequent issues made no mention of the trial of New Mexicans in Utah.

4. "Acts in Relation to Service," in *Acts, Resolutions, and Memorials, Passed at the Several Sessions of the Legislative Assembly of the Territory of Utah* (Salt Lake City, 1855).

5. Daniel W. Jones, *Forty Years among the Indians* (Salt Lake City: Juvenile Instructor Office, 1890; reprint, Los Angeles: Westernlore Press, 1960), 47–58.

6. Hubert Howe Bancroft, *History of Utah* (San Francisco: History Co., 1890), 474–476.

7. Orson F. Whitney, *History of Utah*, vol. 1 (Salt Lake City: George Q. Cannon and Sons, 1892), esp. 510–515.

8. J. Marinus Jensen, *History of Provo, Utah* (Provo: By the author, 1924), esp. 89–91.

9. Leland H. Creer, *Utah and the Nation* (Seattle: University of Washington Press, 1929), 174–176.

10. Leland H. Creer, *The Founding of an Empire: The Exploration and Colonization of Utah, 1776–1856* (Salt Lake City: Bookcraft, 1947), esp. 32–39. Creer, "Spanish-American Slave Trade in the Great Basin, 1800–1853," *New Mexico Historical Review* 24 (July 1949): 171–183.

11. Gustive O. Larson, *Outline History of Utah and the Mormons* (Salt Lake City: Deseret Book Co., 1965), 159–161.

12. L. R. Bailey, *Indian Slave Trade in the Southwest* (Los Angeles: Westernlore Press, 1966), 164; see also sec. 3, "Slave Raiders in the Great Basin, 1760–1855," 139–172.

13. Joseph J. Hill, "Spanish and Mexican Exploration and Trade Northwest from New Mexico into the Great Basin," *Utah Historical Quarterly* 2 (January 1930): 3–23; and Hill, "The Old Spanish Trail: A Study of Spanish and Mexican Trade and Exploration Northwest from New Mexico to the Great Basin and California," *Hispanic American Historical Review* 4 (1921): 444–473.

14. William J. Snow, "Utah Indians and Spanish Slave Trade," *Utah Historical Quarterly* 2 (July 1929): 67–73; Snow, "Some Source Documents on Utah Indian Slavery," *Utah Historical Quarterly* 2 (July 1929): 76–90.

15. B. H. Roberts, *A Comprehensive History of the Church of Jesus Christ of Latter-day Saints*, 6 vols. (Salt Lake City: Deseret News Press, 1930), vol. 4, 33–40.

16. Andrew Love Neff, *History of Utah, 1847–1869*, ed. Leland Hargrave Creer (Salt Lake City: Deseret News Press, 1940), 370–371.

17. Milton R. Hunter, *Utah in Her Western Setting* (Salt Lake City: Deseret News Press, 1943), 305–306; Hunter, *Utah: Story of Her People* (Salt Lake City: Deseret News Press, 1946).

18. Gustive O. Larson, "Walkara's Half Century," *Western Humanities Review* 6 (Summer 1952), esp. 242–243, 249.

19. LeRoy R. Hafen and Ann W. Hafen, *Old Spanish Trail: Santa Fe to Los Angeles* (Glendale, Calif.: Arthur H. Clark, 1954).

20. Joseph P. Sánchez, *Explorers, Traders, and Slavers: Forging the Old Spanish Trail, 1678–1850* (Salt Lake City: University of Utah Press, 1997), 130–132, 173 nn. 306–309. Sánchez collected his quotations from Hill's "Spanish and Mexican Exploration" and Snow's "Utah Indians and the Spanish Slave Trade," and references a trade license granted to José María Chávez documented in the New Mexican Indian Superintendency, RG 75. However, he erroneously interprets the license as an attempt to renew the trade after the Utah trial, despite noting that Chávez's license was issued in September 1850, a year before the trial. He adds that it was Chávez who complained he was "rebuffed" by the Mormons because they wanted to "dominate" the trade. This sounds suspiciously like the complaint that was made by Luján himself when he appealed to Washington about the trial after he returned from his ill-fated trip to Utah in 1852. Luján served as a captain in the Abiquiú militia under General José María Chávez, and the two were probably friends.

21. Paul Bailey, *Walkara, Hawk of the Mountains* (Los Angeles: Westernlore Press, 1954), esp. 124–136.

22. Conway B. Sonne, *The World of Wakara* (San Antonio: Naylor, 1962), esp. 134–139.

23. Larson, *Outline History of Utah*, 159–161.

24. Bailey, *Indian Slave Trade*, 139–172.

25. There were Utes in central Utah who still ate horses rather than ride them. This point was argued by Omer C. Stewart and Julian Steward in the Ute Indian claims cases: based on whether they rode horses or not, were the central Utah Indians Utes or Paiutes? The court found that regardless of their pedestrian status or cuisine, they were Utes—they identified themselves as Utes, and others identified them as Utes. Personal communication, Omer C. Stewart, 1977.

26. Bailey, *Indian Slave Trade*, 160, 163–164. The Utes were considered some of the best-armed Indians in Colorado as well as Utah, a source of alarm to many frontier New

Mexicans; ironically, New Mexicans believed they were being armed by Mormons. See C. Carson to Sam M. Yost, January 28, February 28, and March 31, 1858, in New Mexico Indian Superintendency (hereinafter NMIS), RG 75, T21, roll 1. Carson reported that "Indians from Utah have been . . . requesting their aid for the Mormons" and to "forfeit their allegiance to the United States." Notably, this was during the 1857–58 "Johnston's War," when American troops were sent to invade Utah and put down the Mormon "rebellion," and some Mormons were anticipating using the Indians as the "battle ax of the Lord"—so there may be some truth to the rumors Carson heard.

27. Bailey, *Indian Slave Trade*, 164; the slave trade was Wákara's economic "life-blood," and he was indubitably angered by its curtailment.

28. S. Lyman Tyler, "The Indians in Utah Territory," chap. 9 in *Utah's History*, ed. Richard D. Poll et al. (Salt Lake City: Utah State University Press, 1989), 360.

29. S. George Ellsworth, *Utah's Heritage*, rev. ed. (Salt Lake City: Peregrine Smith, 1977), 210; S. George Ellsworth, *The New Utah's Heritage*, rev. ed. (Salt Lake City: Gibbs Smith, 1992), 13–14.

30. Dean L. May, *Utah: A People's History* (Salt Lake City: University of Utah Press, 1987, 1993), 32, 106.

CHAPTER TWO. THE INDIAN SLAVE TRADE IN NEW MEXICO

1. From *Purchas His Pilgrimes*, 1699–1700, 1908 ed., iv, as quoted in Almon Wheeler Lauber, *Indian Slavery in Colonial Times within the Present Limits of the United States* (New York: Columbia University, 1913), 36; the general summary of Indian enslavement of Indians here is taken from Lauber's first chapter, 25–47.

2. Lauber, *Indian Slavery in Colonial Times*, 31–32, citing Reuben Gold Thwaites, *Jesuit Relations and Allied Documents*, vol. 64, 301, and his *Early Western Travels*, vol. 6, 61.

3. Lauber, *Indian Slavery in Colonial Times*, 33 and 45–46 n. 3, quoting Hubert Howe Bancroft, *History of the Northwest Coast*, ii, 647–649.

4. Lauber, *Indian Slavery in Colonial Times*, 40.

5. Lauber, *Indian Slavery in Colonial Times*, 67, 74, 82.

6. Lauber, *Indian Slavery in Colonial Times*, 38–39, citing *Wisconsin Historical Society Collections*, vol. 5, 79.

7. Many books retell the history of European treatment of North American Indians. See, for example, Arrell Morgan Gibson, *The American Indian: Prehistory to the Present* (Lexington, Mass.: D. C. Heath, 1980), 91–303; Francis Jennings, *The Invasion of America: Indians, Colonialism, and the Cant of Conquest* (Chapel Hill: University of North Carolina Press, 1975).

8. Lauber, *Indian Slavery in Colonial Times*, 76–77; LaSalle quoted, 77.

9. Bailey, *Indian Slave Trade*, xii.

10. Spanish slave galleys were notorious for being manned by English sailors captured in naval battles; other English captives served out their captivity as servants in Spain.

11. See in Kirkpatrick Sale, *The Conquest of Paradise* (New York: Knopf, 1990; reprint, New York: Plume Books, 1991), 96–97, 110–112.

12. Viceroy Luis de Velasco to king, December 17, 1608, quoted in David J. Weber, *The Spanish Frontier in North America* (New Haven: Yale University Press, 1992), 123.

13. Edmund S. Morgan, *American Slavery, American Freedom* (New York: W. W. Norton, 1975), offers a good discussion of this attitude in the first several chapters.

14. Almost all Europeans exploited Indian labor in their exploratory or colonial periods. The Russians enslaved their fur-trapping Aleuts, the English attempted to enslave Indians on the East Coast for use on plantations mainland or on islands, as did the French. And of course, the Spanish are well known for their use of Indian labor. Such Indian slavery existed as late as the mid-eighteenth century, although it was giving way to Negro slavery, which was more profitable. At one time the exchange rate for slaves for French planters was three Indians to two blacks. When Spain obtained Louisiana, Spanish governors tried on several occasions to enforce Spanish laws against Indian slavery among the French planters who owned Indian slaves. Histories of general European exploitation of Indian labor include Lauber, *Indian Slavery in Colonial Times*, and Gibson, *American Indian*, 91–216.

15. For example, Lauber, *Indian Slavery in Colonial Times*, 49–62; Weber, *Spanish Frontier*, 31–37, 44.

16. As quoted in Lauber, *Indian Slavery in Colonial Times*, 48–50.

17. Hafen and Hafen, *Old Spanish Trail*, 260.

18. Albert H. Schroeder and Omer Stewart, "Indian Servitude in the Southwest," typescript, Museum of New Mexico, Santa Fe, n.d., 1–5; Lauber, *Indian Slavery in Colonial Times*, 53.

19. On the institutional compulsory labor laws enforced in Spanish America, see Charles Gibson, *The Spanish Tradition in America* (Columbia: University of South Carolina Press, 1968); Charles Gibson, *Spain in America* (New York: Harper and Row, 1966), 143–158; Weber, *Spanish Frontier*, 123–129; brief summaries in Schroeder and Stewart, "Indian Servitude"; Bailey, *Indian Slave Trade*, xi–xv; and Ruth Barber, *Indian Labor in the Spanish Colonies* (Albuquerque: University of New Mexico Press, 1932).

20. Weber, *Spanish Frontier*, 124–125; Lansing Bloom, "The Vargas Encomienda," *New Mexico Historical Review* 14 (October 1939): 366–417.

21. Weber, *Spanish Frontier*, 123, 125; Lauber, *Indian Slavery in Colonial Times*, 60.

22. Schroeder and Stewart, "Indian Servitude," 4–6; Charles W. Hackett, trans. and annot., *Historical Documents Relating to New Mexico, Nueva Vizcaya, and Approaches Thereto, to 1773: Collected by A. F. A. Bandelier and F. R. Bandelier* (Washington, D.C.: Carnegie Institution of Washington, 1937), 45, 134, 221.

23. Schroeder and Stewart, "Indian Servitude," 5, 8, 11; Bailey, *Indian Slave Trade*, 20–29; Hafen and Hafen, *Old Spanish Trail*, 261.

24. Both Fr. Pedro Serrano and Fr. Francisco Domínguez describe the annual trade fairs at Taos and Abiquiú; see Fr. Pedro Serrano to viceroy, 1761, in Hackett, *Historical Documents*, 486–487; and Eleanor B. Adams and Fr. Angélico Chávez, trans. and comp., *The Missions of New Mexico, 1776: A Description by Fray Francisco Atanasio Domínguez with Other Contemporary Documents* (Albuquerque: University of New Mexico Press, 1955), 252–253.

25. Steven M. Horvath, Jr., "Indian Slaves for Spanish Horses," typescript, Museum of New Mexico, Santa Fe, n.d., 5.

26. Cited in Bailey, *Indian Slave Trade*, 25–26.

27. De Gálvez quoted in Bailey, *Indian Slave Trade*, 66, 30. See also, for example, Bailey, *Indian Slave Trade*, xiii–xv, 29–33; David M. Brugge, *Navajos in the Catholic Church Records of New Mexico, 1694–1875*, Research Report no. 1 (Window Rock, Ariz.: Navajo Tribe Parks and Recreation Department, 1968), 22 and frontispiece; Steven M. Horvath, Jr., "The Social and Political Organization of the Genízaro of Plaza de Nuestra Señora de los Dolores de Belén, New Mexico, 1740–1812," Ph.D. diss., Brown University, Providence, 1979, 45–46, and reference to Ugarte in A. B. Thomas, *Forgotten Frontiers: A Study of the Spanish Indian Policy of Don Juan Bautista de Anza . . . 1777–1787* (Norman: University of Oklahoma Press, 1932), 336.

28. Bailey, *Indian Slave Trade*, xv–xvi.

29. Lyman S. Tyler discusses the early trade traditions: warring nomadic Indians made temporary truce and came to trade at the villages of sedentary Indians in the fall and sometimes remained through the winter, especially at Taos and Pecos. Lyman S. Tyler, "Before Escalante: An Early History of the Yuta Indians and the Area North of New Mexico," Ph.D. diss., University of Utah, Salt Lake City, 1951, 87–89, 98–100.

30. Serrano to viceroy, 1761, in Hackett, *Historical Documents*, 487.

31. Adams and Chávez, *Missions*, 252–253.

32. Adams and Chávez, *Missions*, 252–253.

33. These included, for example, Andrés and Lucrecio Muñis, *genízaro* (acculturated Indian) interpreters and brothers from Ojo Caliente.

34. George Ruxton (speaking of 1846), in *Ruxton of the Rockies* (Norman, Okla., 1950), 130, quoted in Hafen and Hafen, *Old Spanish Trail*, 168–169; and Hafen and Hafen, *Old Spanish Trail*, 265–266. When Manuel Mestas traveled to trade among the Utes in 1805, he met Utes in Utah Valley, as well as the chief Guasatch in rendezvous on the Green River; by this time, his testimony indicates, the trade and rendezvous had become "custom."

35. Examples of trade items included *belduques* (long hunting knives), *punche* (tobacco), corn, wheat, flour, awls, beads, and *bizcoche* (hard biscuits), as well as horses and mules and occasionally armaments. These were probably the kinds of inexpensive goods used by

slavers at the beginning of the Spanish Trail to swap for used-up horses to be traded later on the trail. See Frances Leon Swadesh, *Los Primeros Pobladores: Hispanic Americans of the Ute Frontier* (Notre Dame, Ind.: University of Notre Dame Press, 1974), 54, 236; Fray Angélico Chávez, trans., and Ted J. Warner, ed., *The Domínguez-Escalante Journal* (Provo, Utah: Brigham Young University Press, 1976).

36. Daniel Webster Jones, *Forty Years among the Indians* (1890; reprint, Los Angeles: Westernlore Press, 1960), 49–50; James A. Bennett (1851), quoted in Hafen and Hafen, *Old Spanish Trail*, 271; T. J. Farnham, *Life, Adventures, and Travels in California* (New York, 1849), 377; T. J. Farnham, *Travels in the Great Western Prairies*, 1843, in *Early Western Travels*, ed. Reuben Gold Thwaites (Cleveland: Arthur H. Clark, 1906), vol. 28, 249; Kirby Benedict, Chief Justice, New Mexico Supreme Court, Congressional Joint Committee, "Condition of the Indian Tribes" (May 2, 1865), quoted in Snow, "Source Documents"; Swadesh, *Primeros Pobladores*, 22–23; Virginia M. Simmons, *The San Luis Valley* (Boulder, Colo.: Pruett, 1979), 60; Bailey, *Indian Slave Trade*, 146.

37. A *bando*—an official proclamation—was issued on September 13, 1778, to control the flow of contraband to border tribes; a *bando* was issued in 1812 to prohibit the purchase or trading in Indian captives; in July 13, 1824, California issued a decree forbidding the slave trade. See in Bailey, *Indian Slave Trade*, 141–144.

38. Bailey, *Indian Slave Trade*, 45. In 1850, for example, up to a thousand well-mounted Comanche and Apaches met free-lance New Mexican traders (comancheros) to ransom more than fifty captives, including Mexicans captured south of the Río Grande. Christian Mexicans could be ransomed and forced to work off the ransom costs under the same reasoning that indentured ransomed Indian captives. The reasoning was economic and had even occurred among Englishmen in the seventeenth century; for example, one Virginia planter forced indentures on an Englishwoman he had ransomed from Indian captivity. See Morgan, *American Slavery*, 117.

39. Adams and Chávez, *Missions*, 42.

40. Horvath, "Genízaro," 45–47, 125–126.

41. Horvath, "Genízaro," 116.

42. Horvath, "Genízaro," 118.

43. Brugge, *Navajos in the Catholic Church Records*, 87–89, 92. The effects of Indian slavery on the ongoing Indian hostilities in New Mexico (and Arizona) are extensively addressed in Bailey, *Indian Slave Trade*, and Brugge, *Navajos in the Catholic Church Records*. See, for example, Bailey, 100, 84–86, 177–178, and Brugge, 73, 81–82, 85, 87–92, 135.

44. Brugge, *Navajos in the Catholic Church Records*, 81–83, 87–91; Thelma S. Guild and Harvey L. Carter, *Kit Carson* (Lincoln: University of Nebraska Press, 1984), 233–234.

45. Brugge, *Navajos in the Catholic Church Records*, 88–91.

46. Schroeder and Stewart, "Indian Servitude," 5.

47. Serrano to viceroy 1761, in Hackett, *Historical Documents*, 486–487.

48. Brugge, *Navajos in the Catholic Church Records*, 86, 97–98, 109–112; Bailey, *Indian Slave Trade*, 33–37; Guild and Carter, *Kit Carson*, 135, 222; Lafayette Head, "Statement of Mr. Head of Abiquiú in Regard of the Buying and Selling of Payutahs—April 30, 1852," Doc. no. 2150, Ritch Collection of Papers Pertaining to New Mexico, Huntington Library, San Marino, Calif.; United States Census of 1870, Conejos, Colo., FHL microfilm 545593, Harold B. Lee Library, Brigham Young University, Provo, Utah. All three of the aforementioned Indian agents were agents to the Utes at one time or another.

49. Horvath, "Genízaro," 101.

50. Jones, *Forty Years*, 49–50; Benedict, "Condition of the Indian Tribes," in Snow, "Source Documents," 87–88; Swadesh, *Primeros Pobladores*, 22–23; Simmons, *San Luis Valley*, 60; Steck to Superintendent of Indian Affairs, Dole, January 13, 1864, as quoted in Brugge, *Navajos in the Catholic Church Records*, 87–88.

A comparison of the prices of black slaves and Indian servants yields some interesting figures and is a good indication of the relative value of a chattel (lifelong) slave versus an indentured servant who would ultimately be emancipated; had Indians been chattel slaves, their value would undoubtedly have been much higher. In 1853, depending on size (4'0" to 5'0"), black slave girls sold for $350 to $450, and boys for $500 to $950; infants were often sold for $7 to $10 per pound, making a year-old infant worth between $140 and $200 and a two-year-old about $250. This was several times what an Indian child would have brought. The price for Indian slaves did not rise toward this mark until after reservations and military control significantly cut back the supply while demand remained high. Black slaves in their prime, ages 18 to 30, however, sold for five to six times the price of an Indian, between $800 and $1,000 for females and between $950 and $1,300 for males, and up to $1,800 to $2,000 by 1860. Top dollar went for male slaves in their working prime in the Old South, whereas the top dollar for Indian slaves was paid for young children. And female Indian servants were in more demand than male Indian field hands, owing to differences in the region's varying economy. Indians in their prime were frequently emancipated or soon to be emancipated, surely discouraging high prices on older captives. And, since New Mexicans preferred to raise domesticated Indian servants from childhood, many of the older Indian captives "on the market" would have been "wild," needing to be "tamed," and therefore having less value, as were "wild" or "brute" Negroes fresh from Africa, who sold for half the price of "domesticated" slaves. (Data on black slave prices taken from Lewis Cecil Grey, *History of Agriculture in the Southern United States to 1860*, vol. 2 [Washington, D.C.: Carnegie Institution of Washington, 1933], 663–667, esp. 665.)

51. Two excellent studies of indenturing are found in the following, and data here is taken from the included references. David W. Galenson, *White Servitude in Colonial America* (Cambridge, Mass.: Cambridge University Press, 1981), ix, 3–4, 100; John Van Der Zee, *Bound*

*Over: Indentured Servitude and American Conscience* (New York: Simon and Schuster, 1985), 29–30. Morgan, *American Slavery*, esp. 92–130, has an excellent discussion of indenturing, slavery, and the impact of forced labor on the development of the American ideals of freedom.

52. Van Der Zee, *Bound Over*, 29–30.

53. Morgan, *American Slavery*, 128–130.

54. Bailey, *Indian Slave Trade*, 178–179.

55. Quoted in Brugge, *Navajos in the Catholic Church Records*, 100–101.

56. Older captives, being more intractable, were more harshly treated and more likely to seek escape or return to native homes.

57. Swadesh, *Primeros Pobladores*, 60.

58. Horvath, "Genízaro," 119; Head, "Statement."

59. This happened to eight *genízaros* in Abiquiú who were accused and found guilty of witchcraft in 1763. In Swadesh, *Primeros Pobladores*, 45.

60. Head, "Statement."

61. Captain H. B. Bristol, report on the conditions of Indian tribes, 1865, as quoted in Brugge, *Navajos in the Catholic Church Records*, 100.

62. A sociologist in 1970 found residents of the San Luis Valley, Colorado, who still held memories "which hold firmly to impressions of affection for Indians who belonged to some of the early settlers in the Valley"; people who remembered Indian servants who were "the boss of the house—and we all loved her . . . she ran things," or remember being jealous of Indian "siblings" who "ate at the table and so forth, just like . . . one of the family" and who seemed to be "treated . . . better than us." D. Gene Combs, "Enslavement of Indians in the San Luis Valley of Colorado," Master's thesis, Adams State College, Alamosa, Colo., 1970.

63. Antonio José Rocha, testimony in court action, January 20, 1833, California Archives, Los Angeles I, 115, Beattie Papers, Huntington Library, San Marino, Calif., as quoted in Hafen and Hafen, *Old Spanish Trail*, 269.

64. Rosalio Colom to Getty, June 23, 1867, RG 98, Letters Received, as quoted in Bailey, *Indian Slave Trade*, 129.

65. Capt. Francis McCabe, Report, July 9, 1865, and John Ward to Samuel Tappan, August 4, 1868, as quoted in Brugge, *Navajos in the Catholic Church Records*, 91, 100.

66. J. K. Graves, *Report of the Commissioner of Indian Affairs*, Report no. 40 (Washington, D.C.: U.S. Government Printing Office, 1866), 133–134.

67. Frank Tracy Bennett to William Clinton, February 1, 1870, New Mexican Superintendency records, as quoted in Bailey, *Indian Slave Trade*, 132, 129.

68. Letter to the editor, *Santa Fe New Mexican*, August 6, 1868, as quoted in Bailey, *Indian Slave Trade*, 187.

69. The term appears to have been derived from the diverse inter-"national" nature of the captive Indians, children of many different Indian "nations" who lived together,

intermarried, and maintained a distinct lower social caste; the word probably came from a Spanish adjective that was applied to "a child of parents of different nations." They included kidnapped and ransomed nomadic Indians as well as Pueblo Indians who had become too Hispanicized and were forced to leave their villages.

According to Horvath's study of M. Callendrelli's 1911 *Diccionario filológico-comparado de la lengua castellana*, the root *geno* (lineage, race, progeny) plus suffixes *-izo* and *-aro* yield *genízaro*. Horvath adds that Fr. Juan Agustín Morfí also defined the *genízaro* as "children of different nations who have married in the province." He also notes that recent studies by Fr. Angélico Chávez and J. Manuel Espinoza agree. Earlier studies had also suggested that the term was derived from *janissary* (or *yeni-cheri*, "new troops"), the Turkish mercenary military force that was derived from tribute captives, usually Christian, raised from childhood to be Muslim and to be part of the elite military corps. New Mexican *genízaros*, captives raised Christian, were well noted and respected as valuable military adjuncts. Although a correlation can be seen in the military roles and outsider origins, Horvath concluded that a social ranking based on *casta*, or racial derivation, is more in keeping with the Spanish system of social ranking than one based on occupation. See Horvath, "Genízaro," 73–75.

70. The integration of Indian captives in New Mexico is discussed in Horvath, "Genízaros"; Horvath, "Indian Slaves for Spanish Horses"; Hafen and Hafen, *Old Spanish Trail*, 261; Schroeder and Stewart, "Indian Servitude"; Brugge, *Navajos in the Catholic Church Records*, 100–116; and Swadesh, *Primeros Pobladores*, 23, 39–45.

71. Josiah Gregg, *Commerce of the Prairies*, vol. 1 (New York: Henry G. Langley, 1844), 217–218.

72. Brugge, *Navajos in the Catholic Church Records*, 102–103, 106–107.

73. Horvath, "Genízaro," 144; Swadesh, *Primeros Pobladores*, 190; W. W. H. Davis, *El Gringo or New Mexico and Her People*, 1856 (reprint, Santa Fe: Rydal Press, 1938), 84–85.

74. According to Domínguez, all *castas* passed as Spaniards except *genízaros* (Adams and Chávez, *Missions*, 84); in frontier New Mexico the elaborate rankings of *castas* found in Mexico and Spain tended to be reduced to a simple three castes: Spaniard, Indian, and *genízaro* (Horvath, "Genízaro," 90).

75. Swadesh, *Primeros Pobladores*, xviii; Horvath, "Genízaro," 68–69.

76. Horvath, "Genízaro," 80, 152–173; Swadesh, *Primeros Pobladores*, 39–45.

77. Horvath, "Genízaro," 76–79, 99, 104–105; the early chroniclers referenced here include Fr. Francisco Domínguez, Fr. José de la Prada, and the court testimony of Salvador Martinez, quoted in Horvath, above.

CHAPTER THREE. THE INDIAN SLAVE TRADE IN UTAH

1. Donna Hill, *Joseph Smith: The First Mormon* (Garden City, N.Y.: Doubleday, 1977), 158–161; Dennis L. Lythgoe, "Negro Slavery in Utah," *Utah Historical Quarterly* 39 (Winter

1977): 50–51; Stephen G. Taggart, *Mormonism's Negro Policy: Social and Historical Origins* (Salt Lake City: University of Utah Press, 1970), 15–44.

2. Taggart, *Mormonism's Negro Policy*, 44–63.

3. U.S. Department of Commerce, Bureau of the Census, *Negro Population, 1790–1915* (Washington, D.C.: Government Printing Office, 1918), 1–6, 33–37, 55–57; Lythgoe, "Negro Slavery," 40–54; Jack Beller, "Negro Slaves in Utah," *Utah Historical Quarterly* 2 (January 1929): 122–126; Taggart, *Mormonism's Negro Policy*, 1–73; Newell G. Bringhurst, "Forgotten Mormon Perspectives: Slavery, Race, and the Black Man as Issues among Non-Utah Latter-day Saints, 1844–1873," *Michigan History* 61 (Winter 1977): 325–370.

4. Utah state census, 1850 and 1860, including slave rolls; Bureau of the Census, *Negro Population*, 1–6, 33–37, 55–57. Green Flake was given to the church as part of a tithe offering and worked for Brigham Young for two years before being manumitted. See Lythgoe, "Negro Slavery," 42. Most of the slaves listed in the slave rolls in 1850 as going to California did not actually go.

5. Richard E. Poll et al., eds., *Utah's History* (Provo, Utah: Brigham Young University Press, 1978), 156–158; Hunter, *Utah in Her Western Setting*, 421–422.

6. Before March 1852 there had been no laws either allowing or prohibiting slavery in Utah. Orson Hyde attempted to clarify the church's stand on slavery to British members in 1851 by claiming that Mormons neither forced a slave to remain in his master's possession nor forced the master to free a slave, because national law allowed slavery. Hyde, quoted from *Millennial Star XIII* (1851), 63, in Lythgoe, "Negro Slavery," 50. Although New Mexico would also pass laws regulating the treatment of slaves in 1859 (slave codes), it was only in response to the Supreme Court's having extended de facto slavery over all U.S. territory in the wake of the Dred Scott decision. Even so, the census of 1860 shows no slaves in New Mexico. See Beck, "Sectional Controversy," 139–148; Bureau of the Census, *Negro Population*, pp. 1–6, 33–37, 55–57.

7. Brigham Young, legislative address, January 5, 1852, published in *Deseret News Weekly*, January 10, 1852.

8. Lythgoe, "Negro Slavery," 46, 54.

9. Numerous references in the *Book of Mormon* describe the "fallen" nature of the Indians (Lamanites) in terms of their idleness and blackness of skin. For example, "[God] had caused the cursing to come upon them, . . . wherefore, as they were white, and exceeding fair and delightsome, that they might not be enticing unto my people the Lord God did cause a skin of blackness to come upon them" (2 Ne. 5:21); "And because of their cursing . . . they did become an idle people, full of mischief and subtlety" (2 Ne. 5:24). But the cursing could be removed when "the gospel of Jesus Christ shall be declared among them. . . . And then shall they rejoice; . . . and many generations shall not pass away among them, save they shall be a white and delightsome people" (2 Ne. 30:5–6). (The word "white" here was revised to read "pure" in the 1981 edition of the *Book of Mormon*.) The need to

"redeem" the Indian-Lamanite from this fallen state is recorded in the church's *Doctrine and Covenants (D&C)*, July 1828, sec. 3:16–20: "And this testimony shall come to the knowledge of the Lamanites. . . . And for this purpose are these plates [*The Book of Mormon*] preserved . . . that the Lamanites . . . may believe the gospel and rely on the merits of Jesus Christ, and be glorified through faith on his name, and through their repentance they might be saved."

10. Orson Pratt, July 15, 1855, *Journal of Discourses*, 26 vols. (Salt Lake City: Church of Jesus Christ of Latter-day Saints), 9:179.

11. 2 Nephi 21:22–23.

12. Wákara, or ʻOáqari (*ʔoá-qa-ri*), is a Ute word for yellow; Peter Gottfredson noted that "Wah-ker's" name meant yellow or brass (a yellowish metal), but as a young man Wákara changed it after a dream vision to Iron Twister or Pan-a-karry Quin-ker, or in Ute, Panáqari Kwín'wáyke. *Paná-qa-ri* means shining metal or money in Ute, and *kwin-ʔwáy-ke* is to lie crooked or twisted: shiny metal/money twister. Iron-fisted money twister was an appropriate name for this canny Indian entrepreneur. See Peter Gottfredson, *History of Indian Depredations in Utah* (Salt Lake City: Skelton, 1919; reprint, 1969), 317–318; Southern Ute Tribe, *Ute Dictionary*, preliminary ed. (Ignacio, Colo.: Ute Press, 1979).

13. As quoted in Roberts, *Comprehensive History*, vol. 3, 463.

14. Brigham Young, testimony given in First District Judicial Court, January 15, 1852, *United States v. Pedro León et al.*, in First Judicial Court, "Minutes," located in the Utah State Archives, Salt Lake City, and as Document 1533, pp. 11–13, microfiche.

Wákara was particularly noted for his horse-raiding skills, being infamous in southern California, where he, his band, and a couple of mountain men made it a practice to steal large herds of horses that they drove back to trade with both Indians and American immigrants bound for Oregon and California. Slaving was a product of local raiding enterprises against the more destitute Shoshonean tribes of Utah and Nevada. For more on Wákara, see Bailey, *Walkara*; Larson, "Walkara's Half Century"; and Sonne, *World of Wakara*.

15. Manti, established in 1849, was the second of the two settlements. June 13, 1849, *Journal History of the Church* (hereinafter cited as JH) (LDS Historical Archives).

16. For examples, see Howard Louis Conard, *Uncle Dick Wootton: The Pioneer Frontiersman of the Rocky Mountain Region*, ed. Milo Milton Quaife (1890; reprint, Chicago: R. R. Donnelley and Sons, 1957), 64; P. J. DeSmet, *Letters and Sketches: A Narrative of a Year's Residence among the Indian Tribes of the Rocky Mountains* (Philadelphia, 1843), in Thwaites, *Early Western Travels*, vol. 27, 165–167; Thomas D. Brown, *Journal of the Southern Indian Mission: Diary of Thomas D. Brown*, ed. Juanita Brooks (Logan: Utah State University Press, 1972), 75; Farnham, *Travels in the Great Western Prairies*, 249; *Deseret News Weekly* (Salt Lake City), July 3, 1854; Hafen and Hafen, *Old Spanish Trail*, 261–262.

17. Ernest Beaglehole, *Notes on Hopi Economic Life*, Yale University Publications in Anthropology, no. 15 (1937), 83, cited in Tyler, "Before Escalante," 93.

18. In 1765 Colorado Utes told Juan de Rivera, leader of an expedition seeking a way to cross the Colorado River, that on the other side of the river "there is a species of people who because of the lack of food for their sustenance, they eat their own children" (Austin Nelson Leiby, "Borderland Pathfinders: The 1765 Diaries of Juan María Antonio de Rivera" [Ph.D. diss., Northern Arizona University, Flagstaff, 1985], 212.) Earlier Spaniards had also heard rumors of "cannibals" living beyond the Colorado River. In the mid-1800s a mountain man reported that one of his party of trappers fell behind the rest and was set on by "Pah-Utes"; "the miserable cannibals cut off nearly all the flesh from his bones and carried it away to eat" (Conard, *Uncle Dick Wootton*, 64).

19. Jacob Hamblin, "Journals and Letters of Jacob Hamblin," 1969, typescript, Brigham Young University Special Collections, Provo, Utah, 21, 25, 27–29, 41, 58; Juanita Brooks, "Indian Relations on the Mormon Frontier," *Utah Historical Quarterly* 12 (January–April 1944): 14; James G. Bleak, "Annals of the Southern Utah Mission," 1928, typescript, Brigham Young University Special Collections, Provo, Utah, 17.

20. William R. Palmer, from oral interviews, mss. in possession of W. R. Palmer, quoted in Hafen and Hafen, *Old Spanish Trail*, 281–283.

21. Bleak, "Southern Utah Mission," 17; Garland Hurt, in Appendix O, "Indians of Utah" (May 2, 1860), in J. H. Simpson, *Report of Explorations across the Great Basin, etc.* (Washington, D.C., 1876), 461–462, 278; Utah, Territory, *Acts, Resolutions, and Memorials,* chap. 24 (passed January 31, 1852; approved March 7, 1852).

In times of great distress Indians sometimes killed their children in favor of the survival of the group. For example, during the "Posey" war in southeastern Utah in 1914 a woman threw her crying child over a cliff so that a white posse would not hear it; in 1854 Apaches fleeing a fight with the army drowned a "large number" of their children in the river they were crossing to enable them to escape (Carson to Meservy, April 14, 1854, NMIS, Brigham Young University, microfilm 970.1 T21, roll 1).

22. Young, "Testimony."

23. John R. Young manuscript, LDS Historical Archives, 45, as quoted in Gottfredson, *Indian Depredations*, 16–17.

24. John R. Young manuscript, 45, as quoted in Gottfredson, *Indian Depredations*, 16–18. Purchased from Wanship after a battle with Shoshone chief Lone Wolf, this girl, Sally, lived with the family until Brigham Young urged her to accept the marriage proposal of Pahvant chief Kanosh. This she did, although she was apparently not happy with her new situation. See Madoline C. Dixon, *These Were the Utes: Their Lifestyles, Wars, and Legends* (Provo, Utah: Press Publishing, 1983), 103–109.

25. Arapeen has been identified as Wákara's brother. Most writers have misunderstood the Ute kinship system and have erroneously identified as brothers to Wákara a number of his contemporary chiefs, such as Arapeen and Sanpitch. The fluid marriage practices of the

Utes allowed for the existence of numerous half-brothers, and the Ute kinship system called all male siblings and cousins "brothers" if they were of a similar age. Consequently, in the Ute language all Wákara's brothers, cousins, or half-brothers would have been identified by the single term translated into English as "brother." I have here simply referred to him as a kin brother, that is, a male kin of the same generation. Arapeen was probably a half-brother or cousin. See John Wesley Powell, "Uintah Ute Relationship Terms," mss. 831-Ute, Anthropology Archives, Museum of Natural History, Smithsonian Institution, Washington, D.C., 1873.

26. Jones, *Forty Years*, 53. The Arapeen incident took place in 1852 after the Mexican traders had been expelled.

27. Testimony given at a trial for illegally trading with the Ute Indians for Indian captives, Rio Arriba, September 1813, in *Spanish Archives of New Mexico*, ed. Ralph E. Twitchell, 2 vols. (Cedar Rapids, Mich.: Torch Press, 1914), vol. 2, 478, document 1881 no. 7, and in Hafen and Hafen, *Old Spanish Trail*, 85–86.

The testimony noted the disappointingly small number of pelts obtained on the trip, implying that this had been the major purpose of the expedition; the fur trade in the Rocky Mountains was just getting under way and there was still a lot of excitement about its potential. Other fur-trading expeditions went into the Colorado Rockies during this period as well. Unlike eastern or Canadian Indians, Utes and Shoshones were noted for not participating as trappers in the fur trade, helping give rise to the Anglo trapper and the mountain man tradition in the Rockies. Apparently, Arze and García early found the Utah Utes more interested in the profits of the slave trade than the fur business. Traditions of the mountain man rendezvous are from Fred R. Gowans, personal communication, Brigham Young University, 1993. On the impact of the fur trade on Utah Indians, see LeRoy R. Hafen, ed., *The Mountain Men and the Fur Trade of the Far West*, vol. 1 (Glendale, Calif.: Arthur H. Clark, 1965), and David J. Weber, *The Taos Trappers: The Fur Trade in the Far Southwest, 1540–1846* (Norman: University of Oklahoma Press, 1971).

28. Young, "Testimony"; Utes took captives and sold them to Mexicans or Navajos: Indian captives were sold to Mexicans, and Mexican (and apparently Paiute) captives were sold to Navajos. Wealthy Navajos owned many slaves that could be inherited as property; the most prominent recorded example was Hoshkinini (Hashkéneini), of the Monument Valley, Arizona/Utah, region, who left thirty-two slave women in his estate. See Brugge, *Navajos in the Catholic Church Records*, 76, and J. Lee Correll, "Navajo Frontiers in Utah and Troublous Times in Monument Valley," *Utah Historical Quarterly* 39 (Spring 1971): 160–161.

29. Young, "Testimony."

30. Young, "Testimony."

31. Utah Territory, *Acts, Resolutions, and Memorials*.

32. Jones, *Forty Years*, 49–52; Brigham Young was well aware of the trade. Siler wrote, "Brigham Young said in my presence that the Spaniards have been trading for indian [*sic*] children here in these valleys for years and were here last year and that he knew it. Arapeen says that Pedro Leon has been trading with him for years, and Siapand an Indian who is here says that Pedro Leon traded with Arapeen's father years ago." Andrew Siler to George A. Smith, December 18, 1851, George A. Smith Collection, LDS Historical Archives, hereinafter cited as GAS Collection.

33. December 1850, George A. Smith, "Journal of George Albert Smith (1817–1875). Principal Residence during this Period (1850–1851) Parowan, Utah," typescript, Harold B. Lee Library, Special Collections, Brigham Young University, Provo, Utah, 10–12, hereinafter cited as GAS "Journal."

34. Gwinn Harris Heap, *Central Route to the Pacific,* edited and annotated by LeRoy R. Hafen and Ann W. Hafen (Glendale, Calif.: Arthur H. Clark Co., 1957; originally published Philadelphia, 1854), pp. 223–224.

35. March 12 and March 25, 1851, GAS "Journal," 46–50. According to the history of Zilpha Stark Smith, G. A. Smith's wife, she "raised an Indian girl, father got for her the year they came here." Schoolteachers gave Zilpha Smith credit for raising the child, who became "the first refined Lamanite they had ever seen." Note in GAS "Journal," 85.

36. Brigham Young, May 13, 1851, BYMH, 846, as quoted in Brooks, "Indian Relations," 6.

### CHAPTER FOUR. PEDRO LEÓN LUJÁN

1. *Abiquiú Baptisms, 1754–1866: Extractions of the Archives of the Archdiocese of Santa Fe,* June 5, 1992; Marriage Records of San Tomás de Abiquiú, Archives of the Archdiocese of Santa Fe (Juan Antonio Luján md. María Ysidora Romero on March 31, 1785, and Pedro León Luján md. María Manuela García on January 11, 1826); Virginia L. Olmsted, trans. and comp., *Spanish and Mexican Colonial Censuses of New Mexico: 1790, 1823, 1845* (Albuquerque: New Mexico Genealogical Society, 1975), "Abiquiú"; United States Census of 1850, Rio Arriba County, New Mexico Territory, p. 259, family no. 149 (Family History Library [FHL] microfilm 16603); United States Census of 1870, p. 450, family no. 66, Abiquiú, Rio Arriba County, New Mexico Territory (FHL microfilm 552393).

2. The village of Abiquiú proper was a land grant; land cannot be sold to non-grantee descendants, and even today inheritance of property must be to grantee descendants. Personal communication with self-appointed Abiquiú "visitor's" guide Napoleón García, June 1994. Brief history of Abiquiú in Swadesh, *Los Primeros Pobladores,* 35–41.

3. The official date for resettlement of Abiquiú is 1754; it was resettled again in 1770. The majority of *genízaros* were of Hopi or Pueblo Indian ancestry, supplemented by captives of nomadic tribes (Ute, Apache, and especially Navajo) adopted into the community. In 1779 there were 851 inhabitants. By 1808 there were 122 Indians and 1,815 whites

(Hispanic) and mixed-bloods. The old pueblos, according to San Juan Indians, were *Fe-jiu* or *Jo-so-ge* (*Jo-so* being a Tewa name for Moquis, i.e., Hopis). The history of Abiquiú is summarized in Francis Stanley [Louis Crocchiola], *Abiquiú, New Mexico Story* [pamphlet], n.p., n.d.; see also Swadesh's discussion of the Chama River valley in *Los Primeros Pobladores*, 35–47; Adams and Chávez, *Missions*, 78n, 121; and Twitchell, *Spanish Archives of New Mexico*, vol. 1, 25–26.

4. Stanley, *Abiquiú*; Swadesh, *Los Primeros Pobladeros*, 39–43. Abiquiú, Cebolleta, and Cubero were established rendezvous for slave merchants; these communities were also quick to supply volunteer militias to serve in Indian wars in which captives formed part of their compensation. See Bailey, *Indian Slave Trade*, 100.

5. A *vecino(a)* was a tithe-paying member of the community.

6. Territorial Archives of New Mexico (TANM), Santa Fe, roll 87, f. 115, 128–131; Chávez's license was issued September 20, 1850, and like Luján's was without reference to or restriction of slave trading. (NMIS, RG 75, cited in Sánchez, *Explorers, Traders, and Slavers*, 173 n. 307.) Chávez tradition from personal communication with Napoleón García of Abiquiú, 1994. Abiquiú's baptismal register records only one José Antonio Chávez, who appears to be the appropriate age to have been Pedro León's mother's first husband, and he is listed as an Indian. The only two José María Chávezes who appear in the records could not have been the José María Chávez of the military records (too young). Nevertheless, from the military records it appears that Pedro León Luján and José María Chávez held each other in high esteem and had a long-standing friendly relationship that may or may not have been augmented by a family tie. Although the Chávezes remained prominent, Lujáns are no longer residents of Abiquiú, although the family name continues in nearby *genízaro*-founded Ojo Caliente.

7. Bailey (*Indian Slave Trade*) and Brugge (*Navajos in the Catholic Church Records*) are particularly adamant in their assertion that the Navajo and Apache Indian wars were directly perpetuated by the practice of slave raiding and that slave raiding was often the very reason for maintaining the Indian wars: slaving caused the friction leading to hostilities, and the wars were used as a cover for the purpose of "harvesting" crops of slaves. See, for example, Bailey, *Indian Slave Trade*, xv–xvi, 84–86, 100, 105, 114, 177–178; and Brugge, *Navajos in the Catholic Church Records*, 35, 73–75, 86–88, 135.

8. Mexican Archives of New Mexico (MANM), Santa Fe, reel 22, f. 809, enlistee no. 25.

9. See brief translation in J. Lee Correll, *Through White Men's Eyes: A Contribution to Navajo History*, vol. 1 (Window Rock, Ariz.: Navajo Heritage Center, 1969), 163; original in MANM, reel 26, f. 516–519; report on militia strength, MANM, reel 26, f. 515.

10. Luján to Don Juan Andrés Archuleta, Sub-Inspector of the Rurales, July 19, 1840, as quoted in Correll, *Through White Men's Eyes*, 167.

11. A number of records exist in the TANM concerning the Apache campaign, including depositions and military records. See TANM, reel 85, f. 79–81; reel 87, f. 115–147, 128–131,

151–158; reel 88, f. 3, 2–22. The other three captains were Geronimo Jaramillo, José Antonio Vigil, and Pedro Gallegos.

12. A search of the MANM military records revealed muster rolls and records of the Ute campaign, but Luján's name is not among the militia listed in either campaign. (1845 Ute Campaign militia, reel 39, beginning f. 606; 1846 militia, reel 41, beginning f. 801.) This search was initiated by a remark by a New Mexico archivist who found Luján a "fascinating character" about whom more should be written. It was his expectation that additional information would be found about Luján in a search of the militia records of the major military operations against the Utes in the 1840s and that surely such a prominent militia officer as Luján would appear in the action. It came as a surprise not to find him listed as a member of the Abiquiú militia in that campaign.

13. Andrew Siler to George A. Smith, December 18, 1851, GAS Collection.

14. United States Census of 1870, p. 450, family no. 66, Abiquiú, Rio Arriba County, New Mexico Territory, FHL microfilm 552393, Harold B. Lee Library, Brigham Young University, Provo, Utah.

15. José Antonio Mansanares to Michael Steck, Superintendent of Indian Affairs, July 18, 1864, NMIS, RG 75, T21, roll 1.

16. United States Census of 1850, Rio Arriba County, New Mexico Territory, p. 259, family no. 149, FHL microfilm 16603, Harold B. Lee Library, Brigham Young University, Provo, Utah; United States Census of 1870, Abiquiú, Rio Arriba County, New Mexico; copy of trade license issued to Pedro León appended to the testimony of Brigham Young, *United States v. Pedro Leon et al.*, First District Court, Doc. 1533 (microfiche), Utah State Archives, Salt Lake City, 13. It is obvious that Pedro León Luján was illiterate from the census records and because the court records of the cases in which he was a party (New Mexico and Utah) all have him sign his name with "his mark—X."

CHAPTER FIVE. THE TRIAL OF DON PEDRO LEÓN

1. Trial records refer to defendants as "Spanish." See chap. 1, n. 5.

2. Copy of the license issued to Pedro León, attached to the testimony of Brigham Young, *United States v. Pedro León et al.* The legal requirements for a license were that the applicant be "a citizen of the United States, produce satisfactory testimonials of good character, and give bond in a penal sum not *exceeding* five thousand dollars, with one or more sureties, that he will faithfully observe all the laws and regulations made for the government of trade and intercourse with the Indian tribes of the United States, and in no respect violate the same, and that they will not trade in fire-arms, powder, lead, or other munitions of war. Applicants will distinctly state what tribe they wish to trade with, and under a license granted, they will not be authorized to trade with others." James S. Calhoun, Indian Agent, November 21, 1849, NMIS RG 75, letters received, as quoted in Bailey, *Indian Slave Trade*, 101.

In 1849 no licenses were being granted for trade with the Utes, though obviously two years later this had changed (and Pedro León Luján had been trading throughout these years anyway). A copy of the license appears in Appendix A.

3. Copies of licenses issued to Pedro León and C. A. W. Bowman and of the "blank" license are located in Appendix A. Copies of Bowman's license and the blank license can be found in Brigham Young Collection, box 47, fd. 36, LDS Historical Archives; a copy of Luján's license appears as part of Brigham Young's testimony, *United States v. Pedro Leon et al.*, Doc. 1533.

4. Deposition of Phillipe [Felipe] Santiago Archuleta, January 16, 1852, *United States v. Pedro León et al.*, 325. Phillipe was a resident of Taos traveling with his uncle, Miguel Archuleta, and under Luján's leadership.

5. It would be interesting to speculate whether this was a planned trip or a last-minute decision. Luján must have known his license would expire before he could complete his trading; on the other hand, the Utes told Mormons that they were expecting to meet Spanish traders on the Sevier that fall and Luján was a regular trader with them.

6. Omer C. Stewart, ethnohistorian and court-acknowledged expert on Ute history, recognized two distinct divisions of Utes, those east of the deep river canyons of the Green and Colorado Rivers and those west of them. The eastern Utes included the southern Utes, who roamed northern New Mexico and southern Colorado (Mouache, Capote, and the Weeminuche of southeast Utah); the Tabeguache (Uncompaghre) of west-central Colorado; and the northern Colorado bands now known as Whiteriver Utes. The western Utes included the Utah Utes, who were centered in villages along Utah Lake (Domínguez and Escalante's "Laguna" Indians), such as the Timpanogos Utes, or followed nomadic routes throughout eastern and central Utah. Although eastern Utes sold children to the Mexicans, they did not practice the more institutionalized slave raiding and trade that was epitomized by the western Utes of central Utah. Children sold by eastern Utes appear to have been incidental to regular warfare with other strong tribes. Occasionally, however, they gave away their own children or orphaned relatives to be adopted into non-Indian households, a practice that continues even in modern times (a woman in 1960 offered to sell her infant to patrons of a bar because it interfered with her social life). Utes remember that Chief Ignacio traded a son for a horse, and an 1865 report of Indian captives prepared by LaFayette Head indicated that, of twenty-four Ute slaves, fourteen had been purchased from other Utes. Omer Stewart, personal communication, September 1977, and "The Ethnography of the Eastern Ute" and "The Western Ute," unpublished notes prepared in 1973 for his coauthored article, "Ute," in *Handbook of the North American Indians*, vol. 11, *Great Basin*, ed. Warren L. D'Azevedo (Washington, D.C.: Smithsonian Institution, 1986). (This succinct article erroneously implies that the eastern Utes raided the weaker tribes of central and western Utah; however, the active trade in Paiute and Gosiute captives did not begin until after the

Spanish contact with western Utes in 1776, and it was they who raided these cousin tribes for slaves, not the eastern bands.)

7. Archuleta deposition, *United States v. Pedro León et al.*, 325; First Judicial Court, Great Salt Lake City, February 10, 1852, *United States v. Pedro León et al.*, "Information," published in *Deseret News Weekly*, March 6, 1852, hereinafter referred to as Court "Information," February 10, 1852. See also JH, February 10, 1852.

8. Archuleta deposition, *United States v. Pedro León et al.*, 326.

9. For example, Brigham Young, legislative address, January 5, 1852, published in *Deseret News Weekly*, January 10, 1852.

10. Court "Information," February 10, 1852.

11. Chief Wákara had told George A. Smith in March that he expected to meet Spanish traders on the north fork of the Sevier River later that year. GAS "Journal," March 18, 1851.

12. Brigham Young testified that this took place on November 1, but the other court records and newspaper reports say the meeting took place on the 3d. There may have been more than one meeting.

13. Jones, *Forty Years*, 51. Jones claimed to have been the interpreter for the Spaniards. Some of his recollection of the event seem somewhat garbled, however, when compared with the official court accounts. See also *Deseret News Weekly*, November 15 and December 13, 1851, 45–47; Young testimony, *United States v. Pedro León et al.*, 11–14; Brigham Young testimony, First Judicial Court, "Minutes," January 15, 1852 (the appeals and libel hearings); BYMH, November 7, 1851; Luján's report to John Greiner, Acting Superintendent of Indian Affairs, New Mexico, and forwarded to Luke Lea, Commissioner of Indian Affairs, May 19, 1852, in *Official Correspondence of James S. Calhoun*, ed. Anne H. Abel (Washington, D.C.: Government Printing Office, 1915), 536–537, hereinafter referred to as Greiner to Lea, *Official Correspondence.*

14. Archuleta deposition, *United States v. Pedro León et al.*, 326; Court "Information," February 10, 1851; testimony of F. A. Pomeroy, January 16, 1852, *United States v. Pedro León et al.*, 329.

15. Testimony of Pomeroy, *United States v. Pedro León et al.*, 329; Court "Information," February 10, 1852. No doubt the alternate route would have been the Old Spanish Trail, normally traveled by the New Mexican traders into central Utah. The northern route was probably picked to reduce chances of running into more central Utah Utes.

16. Greiner to Lea, *Official Correspondence.*

17. Archuleta deposition, *United States v. Pedro León et al.*, 326–328.

18. Archuleta deposition, *United States v. Pedro León et al.*, 326–328; Court "Information," February 10, 1851; Greiner to Lea, *Official Correspondence*; by the time Luján returned to New Mexico and lodged his complaint about his treatment in Utah, the number of lost horses had increased from the original twelve to eighteen.

19. Siler to G. A. Smith, December 18, 1851, GAS Collection. Siler's license to practice law was granted October 10, 1851 (recorded November 5, 1851), in First Judicial Court, "Minutes," 21.

20. Siler to G. A. Smith, December 18, 1849, GAS Collection.

21. Siler to G. A. Smith, December 18 and 23, 1849, GAS Collection.

22. Elijah Averett, J.P., and Titus Billings, J.P., to Zerubbabel Snow, December 9, 1851, Brigham Young Collection, box 47, fd. 36, LDS Historical Archives.

23. The members of the remaining company were Phillipe Santiago Chaves (Archuleta), Miguel Archuleta, José Samuel Gomes, Juan Antonio Baldineros, José Albustos (or Albino) Mestes, and Bicente Chaves. The names of the Spanish traders are a little difficult to decipher from the records inasmuch as they were recorded by men who obviously did not speak Spanish and who rendered the names in various phonetic spellings.

24. Greiner to Lea, *Official Correspondence;* Court "Information," February 10, 1851; First Judicial Court, "Minutes," December 13, 1851, 26; affidavit of S. B. Rose, Indian sub-agent, December 13, 1851, *United States v. Pedro León et al.,* 161–162; warrant of arrest, December 13 and 29, 1851, *United States v. Pedro León et al.,* 157–158; Archuleta deposition, *United States v. Pedro León et al.,* 326; Court "Information," February 10, 1851.

25. Information in the following paragraphs is from Warren A. Beck, "New Mexico and the Sectional Controversy," in *New Mexico: A History of Four Centuries* (Norman: University of Oklahoma Press, 1969), 139–148. An in-depth study of this issue can be found in Loomis Morton Ganaway, *New Mexico and the Sectional Controversy, 1846–1861* (Albuquerque: University of New Mexico Press, 1944).

26. Department of Commerce, *Negro Population,* 1–6, 33–37, 55–57. In both the 1850 and 1860 censuses Utah was the only territory or state in the Far West that listed slaves in its population; members of New Mexico's black population were all listed as free, even in 1860.

27. Many of the officials have been considered disappointed carpetbaggers by Utah historians, and their inability to line their pockets the real source of their irritation; although that may be true of many of the officials, some had honest disagreements with the way Mormons ran things.

28. Edwin B. Furimage and Richard Collin Mangum, *Zion in the Courts: A Legal History of the Church of Jesus Christ of Latter-day Saints* (Chicago: University of Illinois Press, 1988), 214–215, 264–265.

29. Furimage and Mangum, *Zion in the Courts,* 264–265.

30. Kate B. Carter, "Seth M. Blair," in *Our Pioneer Heritage,* vol. 2 (Salt Lake City: Daughter of the Utah Pioneers, 1959), 48–49; Seth Millington Blair, obituary copied with "Reminiscences and Journals, 1851–1868," mss. (microfilm), LDS Historical Archives. Blair was also ardently pro-Confederacy during the Civil War. For example, in a letter to a friend he referred to the North as "the old negro worshipping government of Uncle Sam alias (Devil)." See also Jones, *Forty Years,* 52.

31. GAS "Journal," December 1850, 10–12; March 12, 21, and 25, 1851, 46–47, 49–50; and "History of Zilpha Stark Smith," in GAS "Journal," 85; Heap, *Central Route*, 223–224. License to practice law granted October 7, 1851 (recorded November 5, 1851), in Court "Minutes," 17.

32. William McBride (foreman), Darwin Richardson, George D. Grant, Daniel Allen, Jacob Houtz, James A. Cheney, Stephen Law, Guy Keysor, Joseph E. Book, Jos. G. Hovey, and William Jones. *United States v. Pedro León et al.*, 239–240. McBride was related to residents of Manti, where the original arrests took place (United States Census of Utah, 1850). A search of Bitton's index to Mormon journals/diaries found no record of any diaries kept by these men (or their wives) which might have shed additional light on the trial.

33. George Bean, "Diaries," January 2, 1852, mss. (microfilm 920 no. 10), Harold B. Lee Library, Special Collections, Brigham Young University, Provo, Utah, 1. Francis Pomeroy was recommended to George A. Smith by Andrew Siler, and his testimony appears in his deposition, in *United States v. Pedro León et al.*, 329–330.

34. A summary of the court proceedings can be found in First Judicial Court, "Minutes," December 24, 27–31, 1851, and January 1, 1852, 26–32.

35. Seth Blair, "Information in Libel," December 1851, *United States v. Pedro León et al.*, 167–170; First Judicial Court, "Minutes," December 29, 1851, 28.

36. Court "Information," February 10, 1851. Unless otherwise noted, the discussion of the trial comes from these published findings of the court.

37. January 1, 1851, *United States v. Pedro León et al.*, 239–240; and First Judicial Court, "Minutes," 32. Luján told Greiner that each trader was fined fifty dollars, which they promptly paid (Greiner to Lea, *Official Correspondence*), but the court recorded only the one five-hundred-dollar fine against Pedro León, and the case was listed as *Pedro León et al.*

38. Utah, Territory, "Act in Relation to Service," in *Acts, Resolutions, and Memorials*, 160. If they were not property, then holding the Indians prisoner without evidence of a crime would be wrongful imprisonment.

39. On September 13, 1778, a *bando* was issued to control flow of contraband to border tribes by prohibiting unlicensed trade with Indians (generally ignored); in 1812 another *bando* was issued prohibiting purchasing or trade in captives from Utes (again, generally ignored). Reviewed in Bailey, *Indian Slave Trade*, 141–144; also no. 740, Twitchell, *Spanish Archives of New Mexico*, 263.

40. Hafen and Hafen, *Old Spanish Trail*, 262–264; James Calhoun to Orlando Brown, November 2, 1849, NMIS, as quoted in Bailey, *Indian Slaves*, 100–101.

41. Personal communication with descendants of Ellen Thomas, Ute foster child raised in Salt Lake City. As noted previously, Utes had been selling children to Mormons since 1847; in other instances children were acquired as the result of military skirmishes with Indians when parents were killed, and these children were also distributed to be raised in Mormon homes. Notable examples include militia action against Utes in Battle Creek

Canyon (near Pleasant Grove) in 1849, at Fort Utah (Provo) in 1850, and as late as 1866 following the Circleville massacre.

42. Greiner to Lea, *Official Correspondence.*

43. Utah, Territory, "A Preamble and an Act for the Relief of Indian Slaves and Prisoners" and "An Act for the Relief of Indian Slaves and Prisoners," in *Acts, Resolutions, and Memorials*, chap. 24. Passed January 31, 1852; approved March 7, 1852.

44. For example, Jones, *Forty Years*, 54–56, tells of a repeat incident of Mexican traders under the leadership of a Dr. Bowman who were detained for attempting to trade with the Indians in 1853 in Sanpete Valley; Heap, *Central Route*, 79–81, also relates a conversation with a group of New Mexican traders in 1853 who had been "badly treated by the Mormons at the Vegas de Santa Clara" (two of the traders had been jailed) and who said that the Mormons had threatened to "shoot or imprison all Americans passing through their country," for probable slave trading and arms sales.

45. For example, Garland Hurt wrote on May 2, 1855, that he "recommended Acts to regulate Trade and Intercourse be rigidly enforced, because Saints have perpetuated a distinction between Mormons and Americans prejudicial to U.S. citizens," and gave the Gunnison Massacre as an example. (The Indians maintained a difference between the two white, warring tribes of *Mericats* and *Mormonees* (*muruká-ci-u*, or American people, and *mormon-núu-ci-u*, or Mormon people.)

46. Head, "Statement." Lafayette Head, then in Abiquiú, would later serve as Ute Indian agent in Conejos, become a resident of the predominantly Hispanic San Luis Valley in Ute territory, marry into the New Mexican culture, and become the "foster" parent of several Indian children of his own. United States Census, 1870, Conejos County, Colorado Territory, p. 166, family 260 (FHL microfilm 545593). Also Greiner to Lea, *Official Correspondence.*

47. Appeals filed, January 14, 1852, *United States v. Pedro León et al.*, 317–322, and Court "Information," February 10, 1852.

48. Court "Information," February 10, 1852.

49. Court "Information," February 10, 1852; various court documents pertaining to *United States v. Pedro León et al.*, 182–186, 220–223, 272–273, 317–322.

50. Application for new trial, January 9, 1852, *United States v. Pedro León et al.*, 292–293.

51. Jones, *Forty Years*, 52; *Deseret News Weekly*, November 15, 1851.

52. Deposition of James Ferguson, January 9, 1852, *United States v. Pedro León et al.*, 292–293. It would be interesting to see how G. D. Grant justified the "possession" of Indian children by men such as George A. Smith, who had also recently traded with the Utes without a license under an almost identical situation in which an Indian child was bartered for a stolen and butchered animal.

53. Application for new trial and deposition of Joshua Slayton, January 9, 1851, *United States v. Pedro León et al.*, 294–295.

54. Greiner to Lea, *Official Correspondence*; Jones, *Forty Years*, 52.

55. Greiner to Lea, *Official Correspondence*.

56. Greiner to Lea, *Official Correspondence*.

CHAPTER SIX. Aftermath of the Trial

1. Lafayette Head, "Statement of Mr. Head of Abiquiú in Regard of the Buying and Selling of Payutahs—April 30, 1852," Doc. 2150, Ritch Collection of Papers Pertaining to New Mexico, Huntington Library, San Marino, Calif.; Greiner to Lea, *Official Correspondence*, 531, 536–537.

2. Answer of the New Mexico Legislature to Julius K. Graves, Special U.S. Indian Agent for New Mexico, January 30, 1866, TANM, reel 3, f. 205–211.

3. Copy of license given to C. A. W. Bowman by John Greiner, January 22, 1853, Brigham Young Collection, box 47, fd. 36, LDS Historical Archives. A copy appears in Appendix A.

4. Swadesh, *Los Primeros Pobladeros*, 218 n. 36; United States Census of Conejos County, Colo., 1870; Simmons, *San Luis Valley*, 60; NMIS, Mansanares to Steck, July 18, 1864.

5. Hamblin "Journals," 25, 27–31, 39, 41, 44; Wákara's kin brothers, Arapeen, Amon, and Sanpete, continued to barter with "Piedes" for their children.

6. Outside factors had always affected the pattern of disposition of slaves in New Mexico. The Taos trade center, for example, concentrated the distribution of slaves to the north. Shifting alliances and patterns of warfare against the Indians also played a part, as did the spread of European arms and horses westward through the tribes, altering the balance of power and modifying warfare practices. Thus records of baptized Indian captives tangibly reflect the results of New Mexican military excursions against the different Indian tribes, as well as the changing intertribal alliances, warfare, and their own resultant trade in captives. See Brugge, *Navajos in the Catholic Church Records*, 146–153.

7. Baptismal records, particularly early ones, frequently did not differentiate between Yuta (Ute) and Pah-Yuta (Paiute); Brugge, *Navajos in the Catholic Church Records*, concludes that the majority of the captives noted as "Yuta" were probably Paiute/Gosiute.

8. Brugge, *Navajos in the Catholic Church Records*, frontispiece, 30, 35–38, 147; see also discussion of the slave trade in New Mexico, chap. 2. The number of Navajo captives—and necessarily the attacks against Navajo rancheros—rose significantly following the legal actions that effectively cut off the Utah source of Indian menials after the mid-1850s.

9. *Santa Fe Weekly Gazette*, November 20, 1852, 3.

10. Letter from the *Missouri Republic*, from a private letter signed Albuquerque Writer, July 23, 1853, printed in *Santa Fe Weekly Gazette*, November 2, 1853.

11. See Bailey, "Victory over Tradition," sec. 4, and appendix, *Indian Slavery*, 173–212.

12. Indian servitude in California was seen mainly in the mission system, which was abolished even before American occupation. Indian servitude does not appear to have played a major factor in Texas history.

13. In the opinion of Brooks ("Indian Relations," 14), the only reason most Mormon families took in Indian children was their sense of religious duty; often children were purchased even when settlers could not afford to do so.

14. Brigham Young, address to legislature, January 5, 1852, published in *Deseret News Weekly*, January 10, 1852.

15. Young, legislative address, January 5, 1852.

16. Utah, Territory, *Acts, Resolutions, and Memorials*, chap. 24, passed January 31, 1852; approved March 7, 1852. See also Snow, "Source Documents."

17. Brooks, "Indian Relations," 6, 9; May 13, 1852, BYMH, LDS Historical Archives, 846.

18. May 14, 1854, in Brown, *Journal of the Southern Indian Mission*, 40.

19. For a detailed description of the acquisition and treatment of Indian children, see Brooks, "Indian Relations." Hamblin "Journals," 15, 27; Bailey, *Indian Slave Trade*, 168–169; S. N. Carvalho, *Incidents of Travel and Adventure in the Far West: With Col. Fremont's Last Expedition* (New York, 1859), 193; George W. Brimhall, *The Workers of Utah* (Provo, Utah: Enquirer Co., 1889), 17; Brown, *Journal of the Southern Indian Mission*, 11, 14.

20. Brigham Young to Commissioner of Indian Affairs, *Report of the Commissioner of Indian Affairs*, (Washington, D.C., 1852), 488.

21. Dixon, *These Were the Utes*, 103–107; Gottfredson, *Indian Depredations*, 17. Sally was ultimately murdered by Kanosh's jealous first wife. (Kanosh married four times, twice to Mormon-"fostered" women.)

22. Examples cited here are taken from Brooks's study, "Indian Relations."

23. For example, Bancroft, *History of Utah*, 278; Gottfredson, *Indian Depredations*, 91–98. Much has been written about the lack of resistance among the Indians to European diseases.

24. Brooks, "Indian Relations," 47–48.

25. Brooks, "Indian Relations," 35, 38–39, 42. Brooks notes the occasional reluctance of men to take an Indian wife and the inferior treatment such Indian wives sometimes received from other, white wives. Jacob Hamblin, for example, had an Indian wife, as church records and eyewitness reports affirm, yet his descendants vociferously deny it; another young Indian wife ran away after complaining that she was being treated like a child rather than a wife of equal stature with the others. When she tried to return later, the other wives refused to take her back in.

26. Brooks, "Indian Relations," 44–45. The girl was exonerated of the charges of immorality that had been brought against her and retained her membership in the church.

27. Brooks, "Indian Relations," 37–38.

28. Robert Emmitt, *The Last War Trail* (Norman: University of Oklahoma Press, 1954), 39–40. Emmitt includes in his sources for Nicaagat's background personal interviews with Saponise Cuch, who was the son of a close friend of Nicaagat and knew him personally. He was definitely a Gosiute, sold by Mexicans to a Mormon family named Norton, baptized, and

raised in the Mormon church. Mrs. Norton repeatedly beat him with a buggy whip until he fled. Other rumors about his background can be found in contemporary accounts written by biased whites, including Wilson M. Rankin, Thomas F. Dawson, F. J. V. Skiff, J. P. Dunn, Jr., and Sidney Jocknick. Nicaagat refused to surrender to authorities after the Thornburg attack and was killed when troops leveled the tipi in which he was staying with cannon fire.

29. Lawrence G. Coates, "The Mormons and the Ghost Dance," *Dialogue: Journal of Mormon Thought* 18 (Winter 1985): 89–111, esp. 99. Between 1850 and 1890, 238 Indians were endowed in temples, the majority of them Shoshones in northern Utah, but most were not foster children. Most joined the church in the 1870s in the wake of a general disgruntlement that occurred after the failure of the hopeful and messianic Ghost Dance, which more than one scholar has identified as having a synthesized Mormon-Paiute origin with echoes of Mormon temple ritual.

30. O'Neil, "History of the Ute Indians," 115–119; others who were able to avoid the reservation included Captain Joe with some seventy-five Sanpitches and others in Thistle Valley north of Sanpete Valley, another small encampment in Grass Valley in the mountains above Richfield (Koosharem), and Kanosh's band near Fillmore. They were able to escape concentration on the reservation because they were faring better than their kin in the Uintah Basin, owing to their having deeded land and agricultural successes (acculturation), thanks to the intensive work (i.e., tampering) of the Mormons.

31. There is no mention of any sightings of Mexican traders, and of course the major trader, Luján, had just returned to New Mexico to renew his legal battle there. Also, Daniel Jones (*Forty Years*, 54) notes in his reference to the 1853 incident that traders were attempting to "revive" the trade, implying no (or little) trade the previous year. This may also account for a buildup of Indian hostility by 1853.

32. The Bowman incident is described in December 15, 1853, *Deseret News weekly*, 2; April 23, 1853, JH, and April 30, 1853, *Deseret News Weekly*, 3; Brigham Young, May 2, 1853, JH (quoting from BYMH); Jones, *Forty Years*, 54–55; Whitney, *History of Utah*, vol. 1, 510–512.

33. No large body of Mexicans was ever seen, although a band of 150 Yampa Utes from northern Colorado which had joined Wákara's camp sent peace overtures to Young shortly thereafter.

34. The Mormons were, however, advised to treat them "with kindness, and [supply] their necessary wants." See "Proclamation by the Governor," April 23, 1853, JH (quoting from April 30, 1853, *Deseret News Weekly*, 3).

35. December 15, 1853, *Deseret News Weekly*, 2, and December 13, 1853, JH.

36. May 2, 1853, JH (quoting from BYMH); December 15, 1853, *Deseret News Weekly*, 2.

37. Mormons also suspected that mountain men such as Jim Bridger had added to the problem with similar arguments against the Utah settlers since 1850. The Mormons were encroaching on, or impeding, the commercial ventures of both groups as they absorbed the

Oregon/California Trail business to which many mountain men had turned (running trading posts and ferries) and the Mexican trade in Indian slaves along the Old Spanish Trail. Both groups stood to gain if Indian hostilities drove the Mormons out. In 1853, however, the Mormons moved to solve the problem of this outside intervention in their Indian affairs; they bought out the old traders at Fort Bridger and raised arms and drove out the Mexican traders. See, for example, Whitney, *History of Utah*, 515, and BYMH, May 13, 1849, 76, 77.

38. Heap, *Central Route*, 200.

39. Jones, *Forty Years*, 55–56; because of the earlier disagreements with Mormon officials, rumors persisted that Bowman had been murdered by the Mormons and the Indians blamed.

40. May 11, 1853, JH, quoting from Capt. Wall's report, published May 28, 1853, *Deseret News Weekly*, 3. The Mormons considered this desire for guns and ammunition to be strictly military, "to enable him to continue his robberies," and none seemed to grasp the concept that the Indians needed the weapons for hunting and survival as well.

41. It is called the Walker War because it was carried on by members of Wákara's war bands; for much of the "war," however, Wákara was absent in Arizona among the Navajos. See Howard A. Christy, "The Walker War: Defense and Conciliation as Strategy," *Utah Historical Quarterly* 47 (Fall 1979): 216–235.

42. For example, Roberts, *Comprehensive History*, vol. 4, 36–40; Bailey, *Indian Slave Trade*, 163–164; Hunter, *Utah in Her Western Setting*, 305–306.

43. Heap, *Central Route*, 224.

44. George Bean (for Walker) to Brigham Young, May 1, 1854, as quoted in Christy, "Walker War," 217.

45. According to Dimick Hunting, Wákara died of a "cold that settled into his lungs," on January 25, 1855, at Chicken Creek, Utah (in *Liverpool Route*, 105, as cited in Roberts, *Comprehensive History*, vol. 3; see 462–465). Bailey, *Indian Slave Trade*, 170, notes that "the death of Wakara eliminated one of the factors contributing to the slave trade in . . . Utah. Although the leadership of the *Chaquetones* fell to Arapeen, he was never the equal of his brother in playing the trade." Profits waned, and Mormon reprisals discouraged the traders.

## CHAPTER SEVEN. THE TRIAL IN RETROSPECT

1. Although there was no direct threat against the Mormon settlers in 1851–52, Dr. Bowman's 1853 trade of weapons to the Indians was specifically made to arm them against the settlers. The *Deseret News Weekly* editorial of November 1851, however, clearly showed an ongoing fear of too-well-armed Indians.

2. December 17, 1854, Hamblin "Journals," 28–29.

3. BYMH, May 13, 1852, 846. The "Indian Placement Program" devised by Spencer W. Kimball (later revered by Mormons as president and prophet of their church) in the 1950s

was very similar to the program initiated by Brigham Young a century earlier. In the twentieth-century version, however, the children were never adopted and were returned during the summers and after their education was completed (or abandoned). Missionaries actively promulgated the program, and many Indian families enrolled their children as a means of both providing them a better life and (in some cases) divesting themselves of their children for nine months of the year. The purpose of the program was identical to that of Brigham Young's, to acculturate Indian children into the "white" way of life and the Mormon religion, in order to raise up a "remnant of the seed of Joseph" to be a "white and delightsome"—that is, righteous—people. The Indian Placement Program was phased out in the 1990s as electronic media, improved educational systems, and a spread of the Mormon church on or near reservations made it obsolete. The only remaining participants in 1998 were a few completing high school programs already begun or children placed in the normal course of social welfare services.

4. See Lauber, *Indian Slavery in Colonial Times*, 49–50, and Hafen and Hafen, *Old Spanish Trail*, 260.

5. The question could be asked whether or not the Mormons adapted their indenturing act from the New Mexicans; there are similarities, and the Mormon Battalion conceivably had the opportunity to view the practice firsthand as it marched through New Mexico. It is doubtful, however, that the battalion absorbed much of Hispanic culture while moving through the area. It is similarly unlikely, given the Mormons' adamant hostility toward New Mexican slavery, that the Mormons ever understood the enforced Indian labor to be anything but slavery; few Anglos did. Young himself obviously felt it was a unique idea when, in his January 1852 gubernatorial address, he referred to it as "a new feature in the traffic in human beings."

6. See Brooks's discussion of the failure of foster Indian children to integrate in Utah, in "Indian Relations." Mormons equated dark skins with wickedness; both the belief that the mark of Cain was a black skin and stories from the Book of Mormon wherein the Lamanites were cursed with a dark skin for their sins reinforced this prejudice (see 2 Ne. 5:21 and 3 Ne. 2:15, for example).

7. See in Swadesh, *Los Primeros Pobladores*, 41.

8. Most Mormons came from the middle to lower classes of the American North or Britain and had not traditionally come to depend on the services of menials or slaves.

9. Brooks, "Indian Relations," 47–48.

10. Orphans have frequently been used as menials or a source of income. The orphan trains during the early part of the twentieth century, for example, brought children from urban slums to rural areas, where they were purchased for use on farms.

11. Brooks, "Indian Relations."

12. One, of probably numerous examples of freed Indians, was the Ute chief Ouray. No records exist to prove he was ever a captive, but tradition suggests it. Certainly the fact

that he spent his youth as a sheepherder at Taos before rejoining his mother's tribe as a young man argues that he—or his mother—must have been a captive. One of the results of these years of indenture was his knowledge of white ways and the Spanish language. His linguistic abilities facilitated his rapid rise to leadership in the tribe when he attended treaty negotiations as a minor chief and tribal interpreter. His knowledge of whites, especially the acquisition of wealth and a comprehension of the enormity of the white population, also helped him be an accommodating chief for U.S. negotiators. As a result, he would ultimately be appointed by the federal government to be head chief of all the Ute nation. See, for example, Thomas F. Dawson, "Major Thompson, Chief Ouray, and the Utes: An Interview, May 23, 1921," *Colorado Magazine* 7 (May 1930): 113–122; Wilson Rockwell, *The Utes: A Forgotten People* (Denver: Sage Books, 1956), 88–110, 166–171; Ute Mountain Utes, "Tribal Government—Ouray," posting on World Wide Web on March 16, 1997: <aclin.org/other/society_cultureofnative_american/ute/government.html>; P. David Smith, *Ouray, Chief of the Utes* (Ouray, Colo.: Wayfinder Press, 1986), 34–37, 40, 43, 133.

13. For example, Bailey, *Indian Slave Trade*, 173–208.

14. Jones, *Forty Years*, 52.

15. Furimage and Mangum, *Zion in the Courts*, 264–265, 214–215; Eugene Campbell, "Governmental Beginnings," chap. 9 in *Utah's History*, ed. Poll et al., 158–159. Although Campbell notes gentile complaints, they were not universal; a number of travelers on the Oregon Trail remarked on the fairness of the Mormon–dominated courts.

16. Brigham Young, legislative address, published January 10, 1852, *Deseret News Weekly*; Frances Parkman, *The Oregon Trail* (Grosset and Dunlap, 1927), 60.

17. In the Book of Mormon the righteous are depicted as being "white, and exceeding fair and delightsome," as opposed to the wicked, who were cursed with "a skin of blackness" (2 Ne. 5:21), and the dark-skinned Indian descendants of the wicked Lamanites are promised that if they accepted the Mormon gospel they would become "a white and delightsome people" (2 Ne. 30:5).

18. The roots of the anti-Catholicism of the Anglo-Americans and the English (of which there were many new Mormon converts in the 1840s and 1850s) lay in the schism between the Church of England and the Roman Catholic Church and was exacerbated by the political rivalries of Spain and England and of the American colonies against the French Canadians; Maryland was established by Lord Baltimore as a refuge for English Catholics fleeing persecution in England. By the 1840s there was intense anti-Catholic sentiment in the United States, fueled by large-scale Irish immigration and the war against Catholic Mexico. A mass of lurid books was produced during this period which purported to expose the evils of Catholicism. (For example, Maria Monk's 1836 "exposé," *Awful Disclosures*, sold more than three hundred thousand copies.)

Though most official Mormon discourses avoided denigrating Catholics, they were identified as being as idolatrous as heathens (for example, see Parley P. Pratt, *Journal of Discourses*, vol. 3, 38–39), and most members at this time believed that it was to the Catholic Church that *The Book of Mormon* was referring when it prophesied the existence of a "great and abominable church" that would be founded by the devil, would "tortureth and bindeth" the saints, would exhibit "gold, and silver, and silks, and scarlets," and would have "many harlots" (for example, 1 Ne. 13:4–9). This belief was reflected in Mormon writings until the 1960s. For example, George Reynolds and Janne Sjodahl (*Commentary on the Book of Mormon* [Salt Lake City: Deseret News Press, 1955, 1962], 114–115) tie biblical revelations to the "falling away" and the reign of an Antichrist to *Book of Mormon* references to the "great and abominable church" of the devil, and link both directly to the Roman Catholic Church. And up until the 1966 second edition of Bruce R. McConkie's *Mormon Doctrine* (Salt Lake City: Bookcraft) the "Church of the Devil" or "Great and Abominable Church" was specifically identified as the Catholic church. By 1966, however, the Mormon church had taken the official stand that the Book of Mormon references referred not to any particular church but to any thing or organization that was designed to draw the believer away from God (see McConkie, *Mormon Doctrine* [2d ed.], 137–139).

19. Sonne, *World of Wakara*; Bailey, *Walkara*; and Larson, "Walkara's Half Century" provide background on Wákara's habits and favored ranges.

20. Such stories usually form a part of books or articles on early Utah history or the slave trade, including Bailey, *Indian Slave Trade*; Whitney, *History of Utah*, vol. 1; Snow, "Utah Indians and Spanish Slave Trade"; Spanish encounters include the Arze-García affair in 1813.

21. George D. Grant at the home of Seth M. Blair. In deposition of James Ferguson, January 9, 1852, *United States v. Pedro León et al.*, 292–293.

22. Jones, *Forty Years*, 54–56. Jones notes that they took the traders into custody but released them a short time later. If Luján was with these traders (and he probably was), he would have had the dubious pleasure of enjoying Manti's judicial hospitality again.

23. Jones, *Forty Years*, 54–56. Bowman was killed in an altercation with the Indians who had accused him of cheating them. Some non-Mormons attempted to blame his death on the Mormons because of the bitter feelings between them, but Jones offers evidence to dispute this claim.

24. Some historians refer to the Bowman incident first, as typical of the Mexican traders, and then launch into the Luján story as if it were a consequence of the Mexican trader problem. Others toss into this mix the possible incitement of Indians by gentile traders, old mountain men such as Jim Bridger. Thus the Luján trial becomes tied to the general trouble between Mormons and gentiles in the early settlement years, and gentiles are portrayed, possibly with reason, as trying to drive the Mormons out of their settlements by directing Indian hostilities against them.

# BIBLIOGRAPHY

Abel, Anne H., ed. *Official Correspondence of James S. Calhoun.* Washington, D.C.: Government Printing Office, 1915.

Adams, Eleanor, and Fr. Angélico Chávez, trans. and comp. *The Missions of New Mexico, 1776: A Description by Fray Francisco Atanasio Domínguez with Other Contemporary Documents.* Albuquerque: University of New Mexico Press, 1955.

Archdiocese of New Mexico. *Abiquiú Baptisms, 1754–1866.* [Extractions of the archives of the Archdiocese of Santa Fe, database entries.] Santa Fe: Archdiocese of New Mexico, 1992.

Bailey, L. R. *Indian Slave Trade in the Southwest.* Los Angeles: Westernlore Press, 1966.

Bailey, Paul. *Walkara, Hawk of the Mountains.* Los Angeles: Westernlore Press, 1954.

Bancroft, Hubert Howe. *History of Utah.* San Francisco: History Co., 1890.

Barber, Ruth. *Indian Labor in the Spanish Colonies.* Albuquerque: University of New Mexico Press, 1932.

Beaglehole, Ernest. *Notes on Hopi Economic Life.* Yale University Publications in Anthropology, no. 15. New Haven, 1937.

Bean, George. "Diaries." Mss., microfilm 920, no. 10. Harold B. Lee Library, Special Collections, Brigham Young University, Provo, Utah.

Beck, Warren A. *New Mexico: A History of Four Centuries.* Norman: University of Oklahoma Press, 1962. Reprint. 1969.

Beller, Jack. "Negro Slaves in Utah." *Utah Historical Quarterly* 2 (January 1929): 122–126.

Blair, Seth M. "Reminiscences and Journals, 1851–1868." Mss. (microfilm). Church of Jesus Christ of Latter-day Saints Historical Archives, Salt Lake City.

Bleak, James G. "Annals of the Southern Utah Mission." Typescript, 1928. Harold B. Lee Library, Special Collections, Brigham Young University, Provo, Utah.

Bloom, Lansing. "The Vargas Encomienda." *New Mexico Historical Review* 14 (October 1939): 366–417.

Brewerton, George Douglas. *Overland with Kit Carson: A Narrative of the Old Spanish Trail in '48.* Intro. Stallo Vinton. New York: Coward-McCann. Reprint. 1930.

Brimhall, George. W. *The Workers of Utah.* Provo, Utah: Enquirer Co., 1889. Typescript. Harold B. Lee Library, Special Collections, Brigham Young University, Provo, Utah.

Bringhurst, Newell G. "Forgotten Mormon Perspectives: Slavery, Race, and the Black Man as Issues among Non-Utah Latter-day Saints, 1844–1873." *Michigan History* 61 (Winter 1977): 325–370.

Brooks, Juanita. "Indian Relations on the Mormon Frontier." *Utah Historical Quarterly* 12 (January–April): 1–48.

Brown, Thomas D. *Journal of the Southern Indian Mission: Diary of Thomas D. Brown.* Ed. Juanita Brooks. Logan: Utah State University Press, 1972.

Brugge, David M. *Navajos in the Catholic Church Records of New Mexico, 1694–1875.* Research Report no. 1. Window Rock, Ariz.: Navajo Tribe Parks and Recreation Department, 1968.

Campbell, Eugene E. "Governmental Beginnings." In *Utah's History,* ed. Richard Poll et al. Provo, Utah: Brigham Young University Press, 1989.

Carter, Kate B., ed. "Seth M. Blair." In *Our Pioneer Heritage,* vol. 2, 48–49. Salt Lake City: Daughters of the Utah Pioneers, 1959.

Carvalho, Solomon Nuñez. *Incidents of Travel and Adventure in the Far West: With Col. Fremont's Last Expedition.* New York: Derby and Jackson, 1857.

Chávez, Fray Angélico, trans., and Ted J. Warner, ed. *The Domínguez-Escalante Journal.* Provo, Utah: Brigham Young University Press, 1976. Reprint. Salt Lake City: University of Utah Press, 1995.

Christy, Howard A. "The Walker War: Defense and Conciliation as Strategy." *Utah Historical Quarterly* 47 (Fall 1979): 216–235.

Church of Jesus Christ of Latter-day Saints. *The Book of Mormon.* Salt Lake City, 1981.

———. *The Doctrine and Covenants.* Salt Lake City, 1989.

———. *Journal History of the Church.* Salt Lake City: LDS Historical Archives.

———. *Journal of Discourses*. Salt Lake City, 1854–86. Reprint, 1967.

———. "Seth Millington Blair." Obituary copied with "Reminiscences and Journals, 1851–1868." Mss. (microfilm). Salt Lake City: LDS Historical Archives.

Coates, Lawrence G. "The Mormons and the Ghost Dance." *Dialogue: Journal of Mormon Thought* 18 (Winter 1985): 89–111.

Combs, D. Gene. "Enslavement of Indians in the San Luis Valley of Colorado." Master's thesis, Adams State College, Alamosa, Colo., 1970.

Conard, Howard Louis. *Uncle Dick Wootton: The Pioneer Frontiersman of the Rocky Mountain Region*. Ed. Milo Milton Quaife. 1890. Reprint. Chicago: R. R. Donnelley and Sons, 1957.

Correll, J. Lee. "Navajo Frontiers in Utah and Troublous Times in Monument Valley." *Utah Historical Quarterly* 39 (Spring 1971): 145–161.

———. *Through White Men's Eyes: A Contribution to Navajo History*. 2 vols. Window Rock, Ariz.: Navajo Heritage Center, 1969.

Crampton, C. Gregory. "Utah's Spanish Trail." *Utah Historical Quarterly* 47 (Fall 1979): 361–383.

Creer, Leland Hargrave. *The Founding of an Empire: The Exploration and Colonization of Utah, 1776–1856*. Salt Lake City: Bookcraft, 1947.

———. "Spanish-American Slave Trade in the Great Basin, 1800–1853." *New Mexico Historical Review* 24 (July 1949): 171–183.

———. *Utah and the Nation*. Seattle: University of Washington Press, 1929.

Davis, W. W. H. *El Gringo or New Mexico and Her People*. 1856. Reprint. Santa Fe: Rydal Press, 1938.

Dawson, Thomas F. "Major Thompson, Chief Ouray, and the Utes: An Interview, May 23, 1921." *Colorado Magazine* 7 (May 1930): 113–122.

DeSmet, P. J. *Letters and Sketches: A Narrative of a Year's Residence among the Indian Tribes of the Rocky Mountains*. Philadelphia, 1843. In *Early Western Travels*, ed. Reuben Gold Thwaites. Vol. 27. Cleveland: Arthur H. Clark, 1906.

Dixon, Madoline C. *These Were the Utes: Their Lifestyles, Wars, and Legends.* Provo, Utah: Press Publishing, 1983.

Ellsworth, S. George. *The New Utah's Heritage.* Rev. ed. Salt Lake City: Gibbs Smith, 1992.

————. *Utah's Heritage.* Rev. ed. Salt Lake City: Peregrine Smith, 1977.

Emmit, Robert. *The Last War Trail.* Norman: University of Oklahoma Press, 1954.

Farnham, T. J. *Life, Adventures, and Travels in California.* New York, 1849.

————. *Travels in the Great Western Prairies.* In *Early Western Travels,* ed. Reuben Gold Thwaites. Vol. 28. Cleveland: Arthur H. Clark, 1906.

Firmage, Edwin B., and Richard Collin Mangum. *Zion in the Courts: A Legal History of the Church of Jesus Christ of Latter-day Saints.* Chicago: University of Illinois Press, 1988.

Galenson, David W. *White Servitude in Colonial America.* Cambridge, Mass.: Cambridge University Press, 1981.

Gibson, Arrell M. *The American Indian: Prehistory to the Present.* Lexington, Mass.: D. C. Heath, 1980.

Gibson, Charles. *Spain in America.* New York: Harper and Row, 1966.

————. *The Spanish Tradition in America.* Columbia: University of South Carolina Press, 1968.

Gottfredson, Peter. *History of Indian Depredations in Utah.* Salt Lake City: Skelton, 1919. Reprint. Salt Lake City: Marlin G. Christensen, 1969.

Gregg, Josiah. *Commerce of the Prairies.* 2 vols. New York: 1844.

Grey, Lewis Cecil. *History of Agriculture in the Southern United States to 1860.* 2 vols. Washington, D.C.: Carnegie Institution of Washington, 1933.

Guild, Thelma S., and Harvey L. Carter. *Kit Carson.* Lincoln: University of Nebraska Press, 1984.

Hackett, Charles W., trans. and annot. *Historical Documents Relating to New Mexico, Nueva Vizcaya, and Approaches Thereto, to 1773: Collected by A. F. A. Bandelier and F. R. Bandelier.* Washington, D.C.: Carnegie Institution of Washington, 1937.

Hafen, LeRoy R., ed. *The Mountain Men and the Fur Trade of the Far West.* 10 vols. Vol. 1 (overview). Glendale, Calif.: Arthur H. Clark, 1965.

Hafen, LeRoy R., and Ann W. Hafen. *Old Spanish Trail: Santa Fe to Los Angeles.* Glendale, Calif.: Arthur H. Clark, 1954.

Hamblin, Jacob. "Journals and Letters of Jacob Hamblin." Typescript, 1969. Harold B. Lee Library, Special Collections, Brigham Young University, Provo, Utah.

Head, Lafayette. "Statement of Mr. Head of Abiquiu in Regard of the Buying and Selling of Payutahs—April 30, 1852." Doc. 2150, Rich Collection of Papers Pertaining to New Mexico. Huntington Library, San Marino, Calif.

Heap, Gwinn Harris. *Central Route to the Pacific.* Ed. and annot. LeRoy R. Hafen and Ann W. Hafen. Glendale, Calif.: Arthur H Clark Co., 1957. Orig. published Philadelphia, 1854.

Hill, Donna. *Joseph Smith: The First Mormon.* Garden City, N.Y.: Doubleday, 1977.

Hill, Joseph J. "The Old Spanish Trail: A Study of Spanish and Mexican Trade and Exploration Northwest from New Mexico to the Great Basin and California." *Hispanic American Historical Review* 4 (1921): 444–473.

———. "Spanish and Mexican Exploration and Trade Northwest from New Mexico into the Great Basin." *Utah Historical Quarterly* 2 (January 1930): 3–23.

Horvath, Steven M., Jr. "Indian Slaves for Spanish Horses." Typescript. Santa Fe: Museum of New Mexico, n.d.

———. "The Social and Political Organization of the Genízaro of Plaza de Nuestra Señora de los Dolores de Belén, New Mexico, 1740–1812." Ph.D. diss., Brown University, Providence, 1979.

Hunter, Milton R. *Utah: Story of Her People.* Salt Lake City: Deseret News Press, 1946.

———. *Utah in Her Western Setting.* Salt Lake City: Deseret News Press, 1943.

Hurt, Dr. Garland. "Indians of Utah." Appendix O. In *Report of Explorations across the Great Basin,* comp. J. H. Simpson. Washington, D.C., 1876.

James, George Wharton. *Utah: The Land of Blossoming Valleys.* "See America First" Series. Boston: Page, 1922.

Jennings, Francis. *The Invasion of America: Indians, Colonialism, and the Cant of Conquest.* Chapel Hill: University of North Carolina Press, 1975.

Jensen, J. Marinus. *History of Provo, Utah.* Provo, Utah: By the author, 1924.

Jones, Daniel W. *Forty Years among the Indians.* Salt Lake City: Juvenile Instructor Office, 1890. Reprint. Los Angeles: Westernlore Press, 1960.

Larson, Gustive O. *Outline History of Utah and the Mormons.* Salt Lake City: Deseret Book Co., 1965.

———. "Walkara's Half Century." *Western Humanities Review* 6 (Summer 1952): 235–259.

Lauber, Almon Wheeler. *Indian Slavery in Colonial Times within the Present Limits of the United States.* New York: Columbia University Press, 1913.

Leiby, Austin Nelson. "Borderland Pathfinders: The 1765 Diaries of Juan María Antonio de Rivera." Ph.D. diss., Northern Arizona University, Flagstaff, 1985.

Look, Al. *Utes' Last Stand, at White River and Milk Creek, Western Colorado, in 1879.* Denver: Golden Bell Press, 1972.

Lythgoe, Dennis L. "Negro Slavery in Utah." 39 (Winter 1971): 40–54.

May, Dean L. *Utah: A People's History.* Salt Lake City: University of Utah Press, 1987, 1993.

Morgan, Edmund S. *American Slavery, American Freedom.* New York: W. W. Norton, 1975.

Neff, Andrew Love. *History of Utah, 1847–1869.* Ed. Leland Hargrave Creer. Salt Lake City: Deseret News Press, 1940.

New Mexico. Mexican Archives of New Mexico. Microfilm. Santa Fe: State Historical Archives.

———. Spanish Archives of New Mexico. Microfilm. Santa Fe: State Historical Archives.

———. Territorial Archives of New Mexico. Microfilm. Santa Fe: State Historical Archives.

Olmsted, Virginia L., trans. and comp. *Spanish and Mexican Colonial Censuses of New Mexico: 1790, 1823, 1845.* Albuquerque: New Mexico Genealogical Society, 1975.

O'Neil, Floyd A. "A History of the Ute Indians until 1890." Ph.D. diss., University of Utah, Salt Lake City, 1973.

O'Neil, Floyd A., and Kathryn L. MacKay. *A History of the Uintah-Ouray Ute Lands.* American West Center Occasional Papers. Salt Lake City: University of Utah Press, n.d.

Opler, Marvin. "The Southern Ute of Colorado." In *Acculturation in Seven American Indian Tribes*, ed. Ralph Linton, 119–203. New York: Harper and Sons, 1940.

Parkman, Francis. *The Oregon Trail.* Reprint. New York: Grosset and Dunlap, 1927.

Poll, Richard D., gen. ed., and Thomas G. Alexander, Eugene E. Campbell, and David E. Miller, assoc. eds. *Utah's History.* Provo, Utah: Brigham Young University Press, 1989.

Powell, John Wesley, "Uintah Ute Relationship Terms." Ms. 831-Ute. Anthropology Archives, Museum of Natural History, Smithsonian Institution. Washington, D.C., 1873.

Roberts, B. H. *A Comprehensive History of the Church of Jesus Christ of Latter-day Saints.* 6 vols. Salt Lake City: Deseret News Press, 1930.

Rockwell, Wilson. *The Utes: A Forgotten People.* Denver: Sage Books, 1956.

Smith, P. David. *Ouray, Chief of the Utes.* Ouray, Colo,: Wayfinder Press, 1986.

Sale, Kirkpatrick. *The Conquest of Paradise.* New York: Knopf, 1990. Reprint. New York: Plume Books, 1991.

Sánchez, Joseph P. *Explorers, Traders, and Slavers: Forging the Old Spanish Trail, 1678–1850.* Salt Lake City: University of Utah Press, 1997.

Schroeder, Albert H., and Omer C. Stewart. "Indian Servitude in the Southwest." Typescript. Santa Fe: Museum of New Mexico, n.d.

Simmons, Virginia M. *The San Luis Valley.* Boulder, Colo.: Pruett, 1979.

Simpson, J. H. *Report of Explorations across the Great Basin, etc.* Washington, D.C., 1876.

Smith, George A. Collection. Church of Jesus Christ of Latter-day Saints Historical Archives, Salt Lake City.

———. "Journal of George Albert Smith (1817–1875). Principal Residence during this Period (1850–1851) Parowan, Utah." Typescript. Harold B. Lee Library, Special Collections, Brigham Young University, Provo, Utah.

Smith, P. David. *Ouray, Chief of the Utes.* Ouray, Colo.: Wayfinder Press, 1986.

Snow, William J. "Some Source Documents on Utah Indian Slavery." *Utah Historical Quarterly* 2 (July 1929): 76–90.

———. "Utah Indians and Spanish Slave Trade." *Utah Historical Quarterly* 2 (1929): 67–75.

Sonne, Conway B. *The World of Wakara.* San Antonio: Naylor, 1962.

Southern Ute Tribe. *Ute Dictionary.* 2 vols. Ignacio, Colo.: Ute Press, 1979.

Stanley, Francis [Louis Crocchiola]. *Abiquiú, New Mexico Story.* Pamphlet. N.p., n.d. Also bound in Crocchiola, *New Mexico Stories,* vol. 1. N.p., n.d.

Stewart, Omer C. "The Eastern Ute" and "The Western Ute." Unpublished notes prepared (1973) for Donald Callaway, Joel Janetski, and Omer C. Stewart, "Ute." In *Handbook of the North American Indians.* Vol. 11, *Great Basin.* Ed. Warren L. D'Azevedo. Washington, D.C.: Smithsonian Institution, 1986. (Copies in possession of Sondra Jones.)

Swadesh, Frances Leon. "Hispanic Americans of the Ute Frontier from the Chama Valley to the San Juan Basin, 1694–1960." Ph.D. diss., University of Colorado, Boulder, 1966.

———. *Los Primeros Pobladores: Hispanic Americans of the Ute Frontier.* Notre Dame, Ind.: University of Notre Dame Press, 1974.

Taggart, Stephen G. *Mormonism's Negro Policy: Social and Historical Origins.* Salt Lake City: University of Utah Press, 1970.

Thomas, A. B. *Forgotten Frontiers: A Study of the Spanish Indian Policy of Don Juan Bautista de Anza . . . 1777–1787.* Norman: University of Oklahoma Press, 1932.

Twitchell, Ralph E., ed. *Spanish Archives of New Mexico.* 2 vols. Cedar Rapids, Mich.: Torch Press, 1914.

Tyler, Lyman S. "Before Escalante: An Early History of the Yuta Indians and the Area North of New Mexico." Ph.D. diss., University of Utah, Salt Lake City, 1951.

———. "The Indians in Utah Territory." Chap. 9 in *Utah's History,* ed. Richard D. Poll et al. Provo, Utah: Brigham Young University Press, 1978.

United States. New Mexico Indian Superintendency. Microfilm. RG 75, T21. National Archives, Washington, D.C.

———. *Report of the Commissioner of Indian Affairs.* Washington, D.C.: Government Printing Office, 1852, 1866.

United States Department of Commerce. Bureau of the Census. *Negro Population, 1790–1915.* Washington, D.C.: Government Printing Office, 1918.

United States Census. 1870. Conejos County, Colorado Territory. Family History Library microfilm 545595. Harold B. Lee Library, Brigham Young University, Provo, Utah.

United States Census. 1850 and 1870. Rio Arriba County, New Mexico Territory. Family History Library microfilm 16603, 552393. Harold B. Lee Library, Brigham Young University, Provo, Utah.

United States Census. 1850 and 1860. Utah Territory. Family History Library microfilm 805314. Harold B. Lee Library, Brigham Young University, Provo, Utah.

Utah, Territory. "Acts in Relation to Service." Chap. 24 in *Acts, Resolutions, and Memorials, Passed at the Several Sessions of the Legislative Assembly of the Territory of Utah.* Salt Lake City, 1855. [Passed January 31, 1852; approved March 7, 1852.]

———. First Judicial Court of Utah. *United States v. Pedro Leon et al.* Doc. 1533 (microfiche). Utah State Archives, Salt Lake City.

———. "Information" in the case of *United States v. Pedro Leon et al.* February 10, 1852. Published in *Deseret News Weekly*, March 6, 1852.

———. "Minutes." 1851–52. Utah State Archives, Salt Lake City.

Van Der Zee, John. *Bound Over: Indentured Servitude and American Conscience.* New York: Simon and Schuster, 1985.

Warner, Ted J., ed. *The Domínguez-Escalante Journal.* Provo, Utah: Brigham Young University Press, 1976.

Weber, David J. *The Spanish Frontier in North America.* New Haven: Yale University Press, 1992.

———. *The Taos Trappers: The Fur Trade in the Far Southwest, 1540–1846.* Norman: University of Oklahoma Press, 1971.

Whitney, Orson F. *History of Utah.* Vol. 1. Salt Lake City: George Q. Cannon and Sons, 1892.

Young, Brigham. Brigham Young Manuscript History, 1853–62. Microfilm. Salt Lake City: Church of Jesus Christ of Latter-day Saints Historical Archives.

————. Collection. Salt Lake City: Church of Jesus Christ of Latter-day Saints Historical Archives.

————. Legislative Address, January 5, 1852. Published in *Deseret News Weekly*, January 10, 1852.

————. Testimony Given in First District Judicial Court, January 15, 1852, *United States v. Pedro Leon et al.* In *Minutes of the First Judicial Court*, Salt Lake City. Located in Utah State Archives, Salt Lake City, and as Doc. 1533, pp. 11–13 (microfiche).

# INDEX

Abiquiú, New Mexico, 26, 27–28, 53–55, 56, 149–50n3–4

acculturation. *See* culture

"An Act for the Relief of Indian Slaves and Prisoners" (Utah), 100

Allred, James T. S., 69, 76

Apaches, 26, 29, 31, 54, 141n38, 147n21

appeals, of verdict in León trial, 85–88, 116

Arapeen (Ute chief), *45*: and Bowman incident, 14; Mormons and Indian slave trade, 14, 49, 160n45; and trial of Don Pedro León, 57–58, 68, 70, 76, 78, 80, 115, 116; and Wákara, 147–48n25

Archuleta, Felipe Santiago, 64–65, 78, 128–31, 152n4

Archuleta, Miguel, 68

arrest, of Don Pedro León, 69–70

Arze, Mauricio, 49, 69, 148n27

assimilation. *See* culture

Bailey, L. R., 12, 16–17, 141n43, 150n7, 160n45

Bailey, Paul, 14–15

Baldineros, Juan Antonio, 69, 70

Bancroft, Hubert Howe, 10

Barboncito (Navajo chief), 32

Bean, George, 68, 74, 76, 78

Black Hawk War (1865–73), 135n4

blacks, and Mormon attitudes toward slavery, 42–44. *See also* slavery, black

Blair, Seth M., 74, 75, 77, 81, 84, 154n30

*The Book of Mormon*, 44, 145–46n9, 162n17, 163n18

Bosque Redondo, New Mexico, 32

Bowman, Dr. C. A. W.: death of, 160n39, 163n23; and historiography of Utah, 12, 13, 14, 15, 16; Indian slave trade and return to Utah in 1853, 8, 11, 94, 104–105, 114, 116–17, 156n44, 163n24; Jones's account of incident in 1853, 9–10, 104;

and trade licenses, 64, 123; and trading of arms to Indians, 160n45

Brandebury, Lemuel G., 73

Brewerton, George Douglas, 65

Bridger, Jim, 159n37, 163n24

Brocchus, Perry E., 73

Brooks, Juanita, 103, 110, 111, 158n13, 158n25, 161n6

Brugge, David, 95–96, *97*, 98, 150n7

Calhoun, James, 62, 63–64, 79, 81, 94

California: and fostering of Indian children, 37; and Indian slave trade, 28, 141n37, 157n12

Callendrelli, M., 144n69

Campbell, Eugene, 162n15

Carrington, Albert, 78

Carson, C., 138n26

Carson, Kit, 32, 33

Catholic Church, 21–22, 112, 162–63n18

Cayetanito (Navajo chief), 57

Cenis Indians, 20

census records: and black slavery in Utah, 145n4, 154n26; and indentured Indian children in Utah in 1860, 101; and Indian slaves in Colorado, 95; and status of Don Pedro León in New Mexico, 58

Chama River, New Mexico, 54

Chaves, Vicente, 68

Chávez, Fr. Angélico, 144n69

Chávez, José Antonio, 55, 150n6

Chávez, Brig. Gen. José María, 55, 57, 137n20, 150n6

children: comparison of prices of black slaves and Indian servants as, 142n50; and Indian servants in New Mexico, 35–38; purchase and fostering of by Mormon settlers in Utah, 49–52, 74, 82,

175